TEPS in
TEPS

650어휘

박기혁

서울대학교 졸
(현) 메가스터디 어학센터 TEPS 강사
(현) SLA 학원 TEPS 대표 강사
(현) 중앙일보 영자 신문 중앙 데일리 교육 분야 객원 논설위원
(현) 한국 생산성 본부 영어 전임 강사
(현) PTT(Park's TEPS Teacher's Group) 대표 강사
－TEPS의 최고를 지향하는 강사들의 모임

TEPS in TEPS 650 어휘

저자	박기혁
초판 1쇄 발행	2009년 5월 25일
초판 2쇄 발행	2010년 1월 25일

발 행 인	박효상
영 업	이종선, 이태호
기획, 진행	김상호, 조승주
출판등록	제 10-1835호
발 행 처	사람in
주 소	121-839 서울시 마포구 서교동 378-16 4F
전 화	02)338-3555(代)
팩 스	02)338-3545
E-mail	saramin@netsgo.com
Homepage	www.saramin.com

Special Staff

디자인 표지		장선숙
	내지	홍수미
편 집		강윤혜
조 판		한현식

※ 책값은 표지 뒷면에 있습니다.
※ 파본은 교환해 드립니다.

ⓒ박기혁 2009

ISBN 978-89-6049-118-2 13740
ISBN 978-89-6049-116-8 (세트)

TEPS in TEPS

650 어휘

박기혁

사람in
saram
in.com

Preface

영어 시험을 둘러싼 여러 가지 환경 변화에 의해서 TEPS의 중요성은 나날이 강조되고 있고 그 특징 또한 뚜렷이 변화를 겪고 있다.

첫째, 갈수록 문제가 다양화되고 있고 더욱더 세련되어지고 있다.
둘째, 시험을 치루는 대상 연령층이 자꾸 낮아지고 있다.
셋째, 특목고나 외고, 로스쿨이나 의학전문대학원 진학 등 그 쓰임새가 더욱 광범위해졌다.

이러한 세 가지 변화에 발맞추어, TEPS 교재도 다양화되고 진화되어야 하는데, 현재의 교재 시장은 그러한 가시적인 변화에 능동적으로 대처하지 못하는 것이 사실이다. 이에, 이번 TEPS in TEPS 시리즈를 통해서 진화하는 TEPS에 가장 적합한 패러다임을 제시하고자 한다.

TEPS는 참으로 복잡하고 미묘한 시험이다. TOEFL처럼 학문적인 점에 초점을 맞추는 것도 아니고, TOEIC처럼 실용 언어적인 측면만을 강조하는 시험도 아니다. 어쩌면 이 둘의 장점만을 모아 놓은 시험이라 할 수 있겠다.

학문적인 내용들을 풀어가되 좀 더 현실성을 부여하여 실용적으로 쓰이는 영어들을 묻는 것이다. TEPS가 최근 시험 시장에 지각 변동을 일으키고 있는 이유는 이런 장점이 토대가 되었다고 볼 수 있다.

TEPS는 실제로 회화를 하다가 혹은 네이티브가 보는 외국 신문 등을 읽다가 느끼는 애로사항을 잘 해결해 줄 수 있는 시험이다. 어휘력의 측면에서 보아도 실생활에서 우리는 이런 어려움을 겪는다. '단어 하나하나의 해석은 되는데 왜 전체적으로는 독해가 안 되고 해석이 안 될까?', '이 상황에서 저 말은 대체 무슨 뜻으로 쓰이는 걸까?'

그것은 바로 간단한 단어라도 초보적으로 배웠던 사전적 지식 외에 실생활에서는 다양한 뜻으로 활용되기 때문이다.

이처럼 네이티브와의 가장 적절한 의사소통에 초점을 둔 TEPS는 지극히 영어수험과 영어실용의 접목이라는 공인영어시험의 목적에 가장 합당한 인증시험이라 하겠다.

TOEIC이 점수 인플레로 상위권 수험생의 변별력을 상실했다는 비판이 많다. TEPS는 TOEIC과 같은 패턴의 지속적인 반복만으로는 해결할 수 없는 시험이다. 이에 학습자들도 이런 TEPS에 대한 관심과 욕구가 더욱 늘어나고 있는 현실이다.

필자는 좀 더 실용적이고 영어 실력 향상에 도움이 되는 TEPS에 대한 관심이 높아지고 있는 것은 고무적인 일이라 생각한다. 그리고 그런 TEPS를 연구하고 학습하는데, 이 'TEPS in TEPS 시리즈' 가 선구자적인 역할을 하길 진심으로 바라는 마음으로 문제 하나 설명 하나에 세심한 신경을 쓰면서 작업에 임하였다.

혼자서는 할 수 없었던 작업에 언제나 도움이 되었던 분들께 감사의 마음을 전할까 한다. 늘 미안한 마음이 드는 가족들과, 사람인 출판사의 박효상 사장님, 김상호 팀장님, 조승주 대리님 그리고 이 책의 출간에 물심양면으로 도움을 주신 류건 선생님, 신일섭 조교, 윤이랑 조교에게도 아울러 감사의 뜻을 표하고 싶다.

PPT(Park's TEPS Teacher's Group) 대표 강사

박 기 혁

학생들의 자습서와 학원 교재의 성격을 둘 다 가질 수 있게 만들었다. 그래서 학원에서의 강의는 물론 독학용으로도 사용하도록 준비했다.

1. 상세한 해설을 통해 정답을 공략하는 법과 함께 오답을 피할 수 있는 Skill들을 제시하여 좀 더 높은 점수로의 도약이 가능하게 하였다.

2. TEPS의 4대 영역(독해, 어휘, 청해, 문법)과 기준 점수대별로 학습 목표와 가장 효율적인 방법들을 제시하여 좀 더 전문적이고 체계적인 학습자 맞춤형 학습이 가능하도록 하였다.

3. 애매모호한 이론이나 군더더기 설명을 최대한 배제하여 학습 시간 대비 효율성을 극대화하도록 구성하였다.

TEPS in TEPS

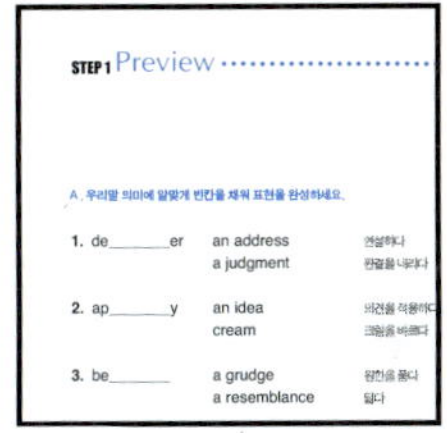

1. 기본기를 다지는 Preview와 Exercise

핵심 어휘를 정리하기 전에 자기 실력을 점검하는 테스트인 Preview와 핵심 어휘를 정리한 후 간단히 복습해보는 Exercise를 통해 실전 문제를 풀 기본기를 다지도록 한다.

2. 핵심 어휘를 정리하는 Word Clinic

시험에 자주 출제되는 TEPS 어휘를 유형별로 정리했다. 특히 〈오답피하기〉에 나오는 가능한 오답에 유의하면서 TEPS 어휘의 빈출 표현을 확실히 외우도록 한다.

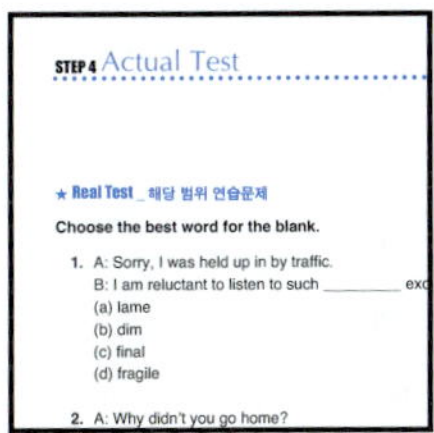

3. 자신만의 해결 노하우를 만들어가는 Actual Test

실전 연습 문제를 통해 실전에 대한 감각을 극대화하도록 한다. 5문제는 해당 챕터의 유형을 확인하고 10문제는 모든 유형을 아우르며 학습할 수 있도록 하였다.

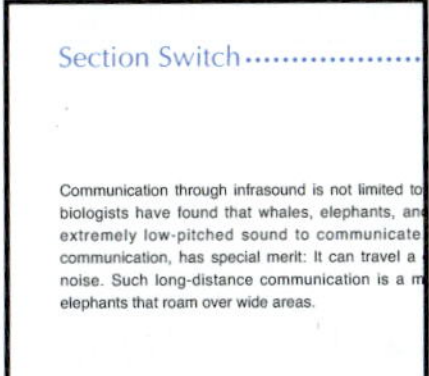

4. 독해와의 연계 학습이 가능한 Section Switch

어휘 영역은 특히 TEPS의 다른 영역과 연계해서 학습할 수 있다. 테마별로 등장하는 지문을 통해 독해 파트에서 자주 등장하는 어휘를 정리하도록 한다.

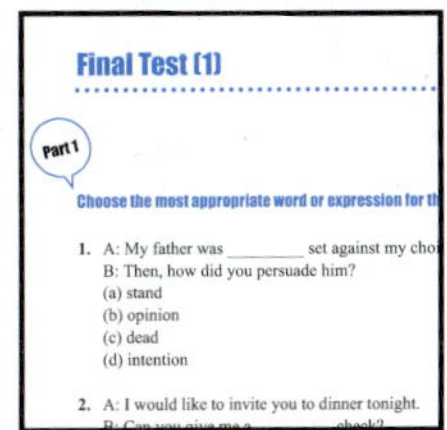

5. 실전보다 더 실전 같은 Final Test

어휘 4회분의 모의고사를 실었다. 난이도는 정기시험과 동일하다. 실전 문제를 통해 정확한 자기 실력을 파악할 수 있다.

TEPS in TEPS

청해 파트의 어휘

토익과는 달리 TEPS의 어휘 시험은 대단히 난해하게 출제된다. 때때로 얼마 전의 독해에서 나온 유사 지문이 청해에 나오기도 한다. 따라서 청해의 고득점을 위해서는 대화체에서 나올 수 있는 간단한 단어들도 정리를 해야 하지만, 토익과는 달리 심도 있는 단어들도 정리를 해야 한다.

어휘 파트의 어휘

어휘는 대화체 Part 1, 문어체 Part 2에서 각각 25문제씩 출제되고 있으며, 출제 유형 및 빈도는 다음과 같다.

Part 1(총25문제)		Part 2(총25문제)	
일반 단어	6개-8개	일반 단어	8개-10개
연어	3개-4개	연어	3개-5개
숙어	5개-6개	숙어	4개-5개
이디엄(주로대화체)	3개-5개	이디엄(주로 대화체)	0개-1개
2어 동사	2개-3개	2어 동사	1개-2개
혼동어	1개-3개	혼동어	2개-4개

문법 파트의 어휘

문법 파트에서의 어휘는 어휘 파트에 비교한다면 상대적으로 무난한 단어들이 시험에 나온다. 다만 하나의 어휘를 중심으로 여러 가지 변형 형태를 제시해서 답을 찾으라는 문제가 주를 이루므로, 특히 동사와 형용사를 중심으로 가장 핵심이 되는 어원과 어근을 숙지해야 한다. 단어의 뜻을 알고 그에 따른 파생 어미의 품사를 안다면 TEPS 문법은 쉽게 고득점을 얻을 수 있다.

독해 파트의 어휘

독해 파트가 비중이 제일 높은 만큼(400점) 특히 주제별 단어를 잘 정리하되, 설혹 미진한 부분이 있다면 다소 추가하기를 권한다. 독해 파트의 어휘는 크게 3대 전문 분야와 그에 따른 상세 분야에서 나온다. 최근의 출제 빈도는 다음과 같다.

	상세 분야	최근의 출제 빈도
인문과학	문학, 역사	★★
	철학, 종교	★
	교육, 대학	★★
사회과학	정치, 외교	★★
	경제, 경영	★★★
	사회, 법률	★★★
자연과학	물리, 화학	★
	수학, 컴퓨터	★★
	생물, 의학, 인체	★★★
	지구과학, 우주, 환경	★★★

빈도수의 분류

★-정기시험 5,6회에 한 번씩 반드시 출제

★★-정기시험 3,4회에 한 번씩 반드시 출제

★★★-정기시험 1,2회에 한 번씩 반드시 출제

Contents

Chapter 1

연어 Collocation

연어란 단어와 단어의 조합이면서도 숙어나 idiom처럼 결합된 단어가 원래의 뜻과 크게 다른 뜻으로 변하지 않은 것을 말한다. 연어는 얼핏 보기에 숙어와 완전히 구별이 되는 것은 아니다. 그러나 연어는 TEPS의 가장 큰 특질을 이루는 만큼, 이 책에서 제시하는 〈동사+명사〉 연어, 〈동사+형용사〉 연어, 〈형용사+명사〉 연어, 〈명사+명사〉 연어, 〈전치사+명사〉 연어를 순서대로 착실하게 그리고 차분히 익히기 바란다.

A . 우리말 의미에 알맞게 빈칸을 채워 표현을 완성하세요.

1. de________er   an address   연설하다
                     a judgment   판결을 내리다

2. ap________y   an idea   의견을 적용하다
                     cream   크림을 바르다

3. be________   a grudge   원한을 품다
                     a resemblance 닮다

4. fi________   an order   주문을 처리하다
                     a prescription 처방전에 맞추어 약을 조제하다

5. fi________   a claim   요구하다
                     a complaint   고충을 호소하다

6. fi________   an arrangement 약속을 잡다
                     a day   날짜를 정하다

B . 다음 중 우리말에 적절한 어휘를 골라 체크하세요.

7. ☐ draw one's appetite 식욕을 잃다
     ☐ drop

8. ☐ stage a nude protest 나체 시위를 하다
     ☐ take

9. ☐ wear perfume 향수를 뿌리다
     ☐ put

10. ☐ heavy cold 심한 감기
      ☐ serious

Answers

1. deliver
2. apply
3. bear
4. fill
5. file
6. fix
7. drop
8. stage
9. wear
10. heavy

650 돌파를 위해서 **꼭 외워야 할 동사+명사 연어**(동사 중심 정리)

administer

administer antibiotics	항생제를 투여하다
administer a drug	약을 투여하다
administer first-aid	응급조치를 취하다
administer medicine	약을 쓰다
administer a test	시험을 주관하다

address

address an issue	문제를 거론하다
address a problem	문제를 다루다

🔾 오답 피하기 capture a problem (X)

address a question	의문점을 다루다

aggravate

aggravate irritation	염증을 악화시키다

alleviate

alleviate poverty	빈곤을 완화시키다

apply

apply an idea	의견을 적용하다
apply cream	크림을 바르다
apply a law	법을 적용하다
apply logic	논리를 적용하다
apply medicine	약물을 투여하다
apply a method	방법을 활용하다
apply moisturizer	보습제를 바르다
apply ointment	연고를 바르다
apply a remedy	처치하다
apply a skill	기술을 적용하다

avert

avert war	전쟁을 피하다

axe

axe jobs	일자리를 없애다, 해고하다

bear

bear a grudge	원한을 품다

◉ 오답 피하기 | take a grudge (X)

bear a resemblance	닮다, 흡사하다

break

break one's fast	금식을 중단하다
break a habit	버릇을 고치다
break the news	소식을 알리다

call

call a meeting	회의를 소집하다

cast

cast a ballot	투표하다, 한 표를 던지다
cast doubt(s)	의구심을 가지게 하다, 의문을 던지다

catch

catch pneumonia	폐렴에 걸리다

cause

cause death	죽게 하다

come to

come to an agreement	협정이 성립되다
come to a conclusion	결론에 이르다
come to a compromise	타협에 이르다
come to an end	끝나다
come to terms with	~와 타협하다

commit

commit a crime	범죄를 저지르다
commit a mistake	실수하다
commit murder	살해하다
commit an offense	위반하다
commit rape	강간하다, 성폭행하다

commit a robbery   강도짓을 하다
commit suicide   자살하다

concoct

concoct a cocktail   칵테일을 만들어내다
concoct an excuse   핑계를 만들어내다

deliver

deliver an address   연설하다
deliver a judgment   판결을 내리다
deliver a lecture   강연하다
deliver a message   메시지를 전달하다
deliver a speech   연설하다
deliver a talk   연설하다
deliver a verdict   배심원 등이 평결을 내리다

develop

develop diabetes   당뇨병에 걸리다

disperse

disperse the demonstrators   시위대를 해산시키다

draw

draw attention   이목을 끌다
draw a blank   허탕을 치다, 헛수고하다
draw a parallel   비교하다
draw praise   칭찬을 이끌어내다

drop

drop one's appetite   식욕을 잃다
오답 피하기 draw one's appetite (X)
drop class   수강 신청을 취소하다
drop the formality   격식은 그만 차리다

evade

evade tax   조세를 회피하다

동사+명사 연어(동사 중심 정리)

exercise

exercise caution	조심하다
exercise influence (on)	(~에) 영향을 미치다
exercise one's power	권력을 행사하다
exercise one's right	권리를 행사하다
exercise a veto power	거부권을 행사하다

file

file a claim	요구하다

◑ 오답 피하기 nag a claim (X) bother a claim (X)

file a complaint	고충을 호소하다, 불편 사항을 신고하다
file a (law)suit against	~에게 소송을 걸다
file (for) bankruptcy	파산 신청을 하다

fill

fill a cavity	충치를 때우다
fill a demand	수요를 충족하다
fill a need	요구 사항을 들어주다
fill an order	주문을 처리하다
fill a position	공석을 채우다

◑ 오답 피하기 A position is possessed. (X) A position is held. (X)

fill a prescription	처방전에 맞추어 약을 조제하다
fill a tooth	썩은 이를 때우다

fix

fix an arrangement	약속을 잡다
fix a day	날짜를 정하다
fix a place	장소를 섭외하다
fix a schedule	일정을 정하다
fix a time	시간을 정하다

get

get a dent	찌그러지다
get the door	(초인종 소리를 듣고) 문을 열어주다
get the phone	전화를 받다

◑ 오답 피하기 see the phone (X) check the phone (X)

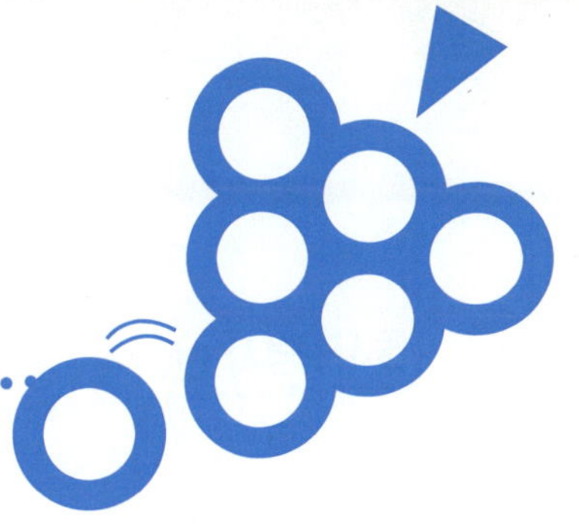

give

give directions	길을 가르쳐 주다
give a holler	큰소리로 부르다, 외치다
give a lift	차를 태워주다
give a pick	차를 태워주다
give a referral	면접자를 보내다
give a big hand	박수치다

hit

hit the book	책을 읽다
hit the road	길을 떠나다, 출발하다
hit the sack	자러 가다

impose (↔ lift)

impose a ban	금지령을 내리다

○ **오답 피하기** speculate a ban (X)

impose the curfew	통금을 실시하다
impose the economic sanction	무역 제재를 가하다
impose an embargo	무역 제재를 가하다
impose the fine	벌금을 부과하다
impose a quarantine	검역을 실시하여 출입을 금지시키다
impose the martial law	계엄령을 내리다
impose a restriction	제한 조치를 내리다
impose sanctions (on)	(~에 대한) 제재를 가하다
impose tax	세금을 부과하다
impose a uniform	유니폼을 입히다

keep

keep an account	신용거래하다
keep a diary	일기를 쓰다
keep a record	기록을 보전하다
keep one's balance	영향의 균형을 유지하다
keep one's word[promise]	약속을 지키다
keep a secret	비밀을 유지하다
keep the status quo	현상을 유지하다

동사+명사 연어(동사 중심 정리)

meet

meet the demand   수요를 충족하다
○ 오답 피하기 acquire the demand (X)
meet a specification   스펙을 맞춰주다

stage

stage a demonstration   시위를 하다
stage a sit-in   연좌 농성을 하다
stage a strike   파업을 단행하다
stage a protest   항의 집회를 열다
stage an exhibition   전시하다

straighten

straighten smile   (치아 교정을 통해서) 미소를 아름답게 만들다

wear

wear perfume   (상태) 향수를 뿌리다

650 돌파를 위해서 **꼭 외워야 할 동사+명사 연어**(명사 중심 정리)

access (to)

allow access (to)	(~에) 접근을 허용하다
gain access (to)	(~에) 접근하다
give access (to)	(~에) 접근하다, 면회 신청하다
have access (to)	(~을) 면회할 수 있다

attention

catch the attention	관심을 끌다
draw attention	이목을 끌다
give attention	주의를 기울이다
merit attention	주의를 기울일 만하다
pay attention	주목하다

budget

cut the budget	예산을 삭감하다

call

expect a call	전화나 요청을 기대하다
make a call	전화를 하다
take a call	(돌려준) 전화를 받다

chance

pass (up) a chance	기회를 놓치다
stand a chance (of)	(~의) 가능성[승산]이 있다
take a chance	모험을 하다

channel

change channels	채널을 바꾸다

○ 오답 피하기 move channesl (X) control channels (X)

crime

deter crime	범죄를 방지하다

damage

do damage	손해를 끼치다, 피해를 주다

동사+명사 연어(명사 중심 정리)

debate
rekindle debate — 다시 논쟁거리를 만들다

degree
get a degree — 학위를 취득하다

difference
hammer out difference — 의견차를 끈기 있게 해결하다
iron out difference — 이견을 조정하다
tell the difference — 차이점을 구별하다

goal
score a goal — 목표를 잡다

knowledge
amass knowledge — 지식을 축적하다

message
post a message — (게시판 등에) 메시지를 남기다
put up a message — (게시판 등에) 메시지를 남기다

name
blacken someone's name — ~의 이름을 더럽히다

sign
show a sign — 징조를 보이다

suspect
frisk a suspect — 용의자의 몸을 수색하다

war
avert war — 전쟁을 피하다
wage war — 전쟁을 일으키다

650 돌파를 위해서 **꼭 외워야 할 동사+형용사 연어**(동사 중심 정리)

break
break loose	탈옥하다, 도망치다

come
come clean	자백하다

get
get better	호전되다
get cute	까불다
get dark	어두워지다
get fat	살이 찌다
get going	가다

◐ 오답 피하기 let reach (X)

get light	불을 밝히다
get narrow	좁아지다
get nasty	더러워지다
get plastered	깁스하다

◐ 오답 피하기 get framed (X)

get shocked	충격을 받다
get thin	날씬해지다, 살이 빠지다
get upset	화가 나다
get well	상태가 호전되다
get bigger	영역이 확대되다
get worse	상태가 악화되다

go
go amiss	(일이) 틀어지다, 잘못되다
go bad	썩다, 상하다
go berserk	광포해지다, 흉포해지다
go blind	실명시키다, 사정도 모르고 일에 착수하다, 계획 없이 무모하게 시도하다
go broke	파산하다
go bust	파산하다
go crazy	미쳐버리다
go dead	고장 나다
go deaf	귀머거리가 되다
go flat	(타이어가) 바람이 빠지다

go mad	미치광이가 되다
go numb	감각을 잃어버리다
go overboard	배에서 뛰어내리다
go sightseeing	관광하다
go sour	시어지다
go steady (with)	(~와) 사귀다
go wrong	잘못되다

hold

hold responsible	책임을 지다(주로 수동태로)
hold strong	강세를 유지하다

keep

keep busy	바쁘다
keep current	현 상태를 유지하다

let

let loose	놓아주다

strike

strike dumb	충격을 가하다

650 돌파를 위해서 **꼭 외워야 할 형용사+명사 연어**(형용사 중심 정리)

acting
acting president 대통령/사장 권한대행

big
big fan 열렬한 팬
○ 오답 피하기 huge fan (X) giant fan (X) great fan (X)
big industry 규모가 큰 산업
big mouth 허풍쟁이

born
born cripple 선천성 불구

broad
broad daylight 벌건 대낮에

cardiac
cardiac arrest 심장마비

close
close acquaintance 가깝게 아는 사람

collective
collective egoism 집단 이기주의

complete
complete novice 완전 초보

current
current affair 시사 (문제)

forbidden
forbidden fruit 금단의 열매

foreign
foreign currency 외화

hard
hard cash   현금, 현찰

haunting
haunting melody   머릿속에 계속 맴도는 멜로디

heavy
heavy burden   과중한 부담
heavy cold   심한 감기
   ○ 오답 피하기 serious cold (X)
heavy drinker   애주가, 술고래
heavy load   무거운 짐
heavy rain   폭우
heavy schedule   촉박한 일정
heavy sleeper   잠귀가 어두운 사람
heavy snow   대설
heavy traffic   교통혼잡

hectic
hectic schedule   분주한 스케줄

inclement
inclement weather   악천후

lasting
lasting impression   오래가는 인상

live
live coverage   생방송

manned
manned spacecraft   유인 우주선

religious
religious persecution   종교적 박해

steadfast

steadfast support　　　변함없는 지지

strong

strong likelihood　　　높은 가능성

650 돌파를 위해서 꼭 외워야 할 형용사+명사 연어(명사 중심 정리)

angle
acute angle	예각
obtuse angle	둔각
right angle	직각

answer
affirmative answer	긍정적인 답
definitive answer	확답

area
affected area   피해 지역

◐ 오답 피하기 influenced area (X)

chief area   주 영역, 주 분야(of interest까지 결합)

◐ 오답 피하기 best area (X)

art
culinary art	요리법
healing art	치료법
martial art	무술

artillery
long-range artillery   장거리 포

case
convertible case   역의 경우

character
national character   국민성

checkup
medical checkup   건강검진

delinquency
juvenile delinquency   청소년 비행

downpour

torrential downpour	호우
heavy downpour	폭우
severe downpour	폭우

drinker

compulsive drinker	알코올 중독자(alcoholic)

effect

after effect	후유증
cumulative effect	누적 효과
side effect	부작용

excuse

flimsy excuse	속보이는 변명
lame excuse	궁색한 변명, 뻔한 변명

◐ 오답 피하기 | fragile excuse (X) dim excuse (X)

weak excuse	궁색한 변명

exercise

military exercise	군사 훈련

eye

naked eye	육안

family

immediate family	직계 가족

fee

late fee	연체료

figure

astronomical figure	천문학적 수치

flavor

subtle flavor	미묘한 맛

형용사+명사 연어(명사 중심 정리)

force

unlawful force 비합법적인 무력

habit

dietry habit 식습관

ingrained habit 고질적인 버릇

industry

big industry 규모가 큰 산업

booming industry 번창하는 산업

interest

vested interest 기득권

job

odd job 임시직

life

aquatic life 해양 생물

punishment

corporeal punishment 체벌

subject

compulsory subject 필수 과목

twin

identical twin 일란성 쌍둥이

오답 피하기 homogeneous (X)

650 돌파를 위해서 꼭 외워야 할 명사+명사 연어

accident
hit-and-run accident   뺑소니 사고

billing
billing cycle   청구 주기

bone
bone marrow   골수

bottom
bottom line   요점, 핵심

brand
brand awareness   브랜드 인지도
> 오답 피하기 brand consciousness (X)

camera
security camera   감시 카메라

courtesy
courtesy bus   (고객 서비스용) 무료 버스
courtesy call   예절을 갖춘 방문
telephone courtesy   전화 예절

fitness
fitness level   신체 건강 수준

food
food additive   식품 첨가제

friend
childhood friend   소꿉친구

fund
charity fund   자선 기금
slush fund   한탕주의 펀드

명사+명사 연어

grass
grass root   풀뿌리 민주주의, 대중

job
rush job   급한 일

language
sign language   수화

program
pilot program   시험 프로그램

rate
birth rate   출산율
literacy rate   비문맹율
unemployment rate   실업률
crime rate   범죄율

seat
aisle seat   통로쪽 좌석
priority seat   노약자석

session
review session   복습 시간

shock
culture shock   문화 충격

store
hardware store   철물점

test
test result   검사 결과

boarding time 탑승 시간
company time 근무 시간

weather

weather forecast 일기예보

wire

wire transfer 온라인 송금

650 돌파를 위해서 꼭 외워야 할 전치사+명사 연어(전치사 중심 정리)

at

at the back   뒤에서 도와주는

beside

beside the point   주제를 벗어나서

by

by sight   얼굴로만 (알고 지내다)

◐ 오답 피하기 by face (X)

for

for ages   오랫동안
for kicks   재미삼아

in

in (a) cast   깁스하여
in command of   지휘하여
in handy   편리하게
in a heartbeat   한순간에
in the mood   ~하고 싶은 기분[상태]에 있는
in motion   움직이고 있는
in (one's) presence   (~의) 면전에서

◐ 오답 피하기 in (one's) front (X) in (one's) nose (X) in (one's) eyes (X)

in shape   건강하게
in vain   허사로, 수포로

off

off hand   즉석에서
off limits   금지 구역의

on

on (the) agenda   의제가 되고 있는
on average   평균적으로
on a diet   다이어트 중인
on edge   초조하여

on (the) go   쉴 새 없이 일하는, 계속 진행 중인

○ 오답 피하기 on (the) drive (X) on (the) ride (X) on (the) turn (X)

on (the) loose   도망 중인

A. 다음 문장에 어울리는 어휘를 고르세요.

1. More desperately, the drought has been going on (affected / influenced) area.
더욱 더 절망스럽게도 가뭄이 피해 지역에 계속되고 있었다.

2. I know the relative by (sight / face).
나는 그 친척을 얼굴로만 알고 지낸다.

3. The U.S. Government would preemptively impose (a quarantine / a medicine).
미국 정부는 선제적으로 검역을 실시할 것이다.

B. 둘 중 우리말에 적절한 어휘를 골라 체크하세요.

4. ☐ affirmative answer 확답
☐ definitive

5. food ☐ additive 식품 첨가제
☐ addictive

6. brand ☐ awareness 브랜드 인지도
☐ consciousness

Answers
1. affected
2. sight
3. a quarantine
4. definitive
5. additive
6. awareness

★ **Real Test** _ 해당 범위 연습문제

Choose the best word for the blank.

1. A: Sorry, I was held up in by traffic.
   B: I am reluctant to listen to such __________ excuses anymore.
   (a) lame
   (b) dim
   (c) final
   (d) fragile

2. A: Why didn't you go home?
   B: I'm __________ a call from my friend.
   (a) desiring
   (b) anticipating
   (c) expecting
   (d) answering

3. In a democratic society, more citizens should __________ their power as voters.
   (a) exercise
   (b) work out
   (c) put
   (d) make

4. Copies of all receipts and warranties are needed when __________ a complaint with the Better Business Bureau.
   (a) saying
   (b) nagging
   (c) filing
   (d) bothering

5. The cease-fire agreement __________ a ban on the use of antipersonnel landmines except in demilitarized zones.
   (a) occurs
   (b) creates
   (c) imposes
   (d) speculate

★Random Test _ 모든 범위의 연습문제

Choose the best word for the blank.

6. A: Can I recommend you about opening a __________ account?
   B: Nice to hear it. Then I can use it with my mom altogether.
   (a) joint
   (b) savings
   (c) sales
   (d) cost

7. A: How was your weekend, Trent?
   B: Great! The embassy __________ a big party to celebrate Australia's Independence Day.
   (a) threw
   (b) went
   (c) marked
   (d) came

8. I took __________ with him on a number of his comments, which I thought were unfair.
   (a) challenge
   (b) offence
   (c) issue
   (d) expectation

9. The Russian government is trying desperately to __________ an agreement to finance its debts.
   (a) make up
   (b) hand over
   (c) sign up
   (d) work out

10. With this password, anyone is able to gain __________ to confidential corporate information.
   (a) access
   (b) excess
   (c) hold
   (d) reach

11. The students __________ a demonstration in front of the embassy to protest unfair
trade practices.
(a) performed
(b) did
(c) staged
(d) made

12. Her brilliant ideas have __________ a lot of attention in the scientific community.
(a) drawn
(b) depended
(c) missed
(d) proceeded

13. A computer virus may destroy data right away or lie dormant and __________ its
damage later.
(a) strike
(b) do
(c) make
(d) gain

14. In order to reach an agreement they need to __________ out their differences.
(a) trade
(b) negotiate
(c) liberate
(d) hammer

15. Visit your family doctor a couple of weeks before going on vacation to avoid
__________ sick during your travels.
(a) turning
(b) coming
(c) falling
(d) making

Section Switch 

Communication through infrasound is not limited to giraffes. Over the last few decades, biologists have found that whales, elephants, and some other animals also use this extremely low-pitched sound to communicate. This infrasound, as a means of communication, has special merit: It can travel a greater distance than higher-pitched noise. Such long-distance communication is a must for animals such as giraffes or elephants that roam over wide areas.

Translation

초저주파음을 통한 의사소통은 기린에게만 해당되는 것은 아니다. 지난 수십 년에 걸쳐 생물학자들은 고래와 코끼리 그리고 몇몇 다른 동물들도 의사소통을 하기 위해 초저음을 사용한다는 것을 알게 되었다. 의사소통의 수단으로서 이 초저주파음은 특별한 장점을 갖고 있는데, 그 소리는 고음보다 훨씬 더 먼 거리를 갈 수 있다는 점이다. 그와 같은 원거리 의사소통은 넓은 지역을 돌아다니는 기린이나 코끼리 같은 동물들에게는 필수적이다.

Vocabulary

infrasound 초저주파 불기청음
be limited to ~로 제한되다
decade 10년
low-pitched 저음의
as a means of ~의 수단으로서
merit 이점, 장점
must 필수
roam (정처 없이) 돌아다니다

숙어(1)

숙어란 단어와 단어의 조합이면서도 연어와는 달리 결합된 단어들이 가지는 일체적 의미가 원래의 뜻과는 크게 다른 뜻으로 변하여 사용되는 것을 말한다. 예를 들어, apply the ointment와 같은 연어의 경우에는 '연고를 바르다' 라는 의미이지만, 사실은 apply가 '적용하다' 의 1차적 의미에서 벗어나 무엇인가 물질을 '얇게 바르다' 는 의미를 가진 것으로 변화해서 적용한 것일 뿐이고, 또한 '바르다' 랑 관련된 많은 표현 중에서 유독 ointment만은 apply랑 같이 결합해서 이런 의미를 가지게 됨을 보여준다.

이와 다르게 숙어는 하나의 단어들이 결합해서 전혀 새로운 뜻을 만들어내는 경우이다. 예를 들어, bring the bacon(생계를 꾸려나가다)이란 숙어를 보면 bacon에는 원래 생계라는 부차적 의미가 들어 있지는 않다. 그러나 상식적으로 서양인들의 아침으로 먹는 주식이 bacon이다 보니 우리나라 말에서의 밥벌이처럼 그러한 양식으로 굳어진 것이다.

숙어는 다양한 방식의 암기가 생명이다. 따라서 이번 Chapter와 다음 Chapter에서 제시하는 숙어를 주제별 그리고 키워드별로 잘 숙지하기 바란다.

A. 우리말에 맞는 적절한 어휘를 골라 체크하세요.

1. a force to be ☐ beckoned with 무시 못 할 존재
　　　　　　　 ☐ reckoned

2. on the ☐ blink 고장이 나서
　　　　 ☐ brink

3. drink like a ☐ fish 술을 물 마시듯 마시다
　　　　　　　 ☐ horse

4. ☐ divisive second 순간
　 ☐ split

5. ☐ carry the day 승리하다, 이기다
　 ☐ take

B. 다음 숙어 표현에 알맞은 우리말을 골라 체크하세요.

6. pop the question ⓐ 청혼하다
　　　　　　　　 ⓑ 돌발 질문을 던지다

7. penny pincher ⓐ 수선공
　　　　　　 ⓑ 구두쇠

8. one's cup of tea ⓐ 좋아하는 타입
　　　　　　　 ⓑ 하기 쉬운 일

9. have a bone to pick ⓐ 말에 뼈가 있다
　　　　　　　　 ⓑ 할 말이 있다

10. have a field day with something ⓐ 야외 활동을 하다
　　　　　　　　　　　　　 ⓑ ~하느라 신이 나다

Answers

1. reckoned
2. blink
3. fish
4. split
5. carry
6. a
7. b
8. a
9. b
10. b

650 돌파를 위해서 꼭 외워야 할 숙어(ㄱ - ㅅ까지)

가까스로
by a narrow margin
간신히, 가까스로

가난
on a shoestring
절약해서, 곤궁하게

거물
a force to be reckoned with
무시 못 할 존재

거절
shut the door
거절하다

건배
propose a toast
건배하다

결심
come to the crunch
결심할 시간이 오다

결혼
be engaged to
~와 약혼하다 *cf.* be married to ~와 결혼하다
tie the knot
결혼하다
pop the question
청혼하다

경악
take someone by surprise
~를 놀라게 하다

고장
break down
고장 나다(be out of order); 분류하다(classify)
on the blink
고장이 나서(not working properly); 몸 상태가 좋지 않은(under the weather)
◑ 오답 피하기 on the blank (X) on the brink (X)

고통, 곤란
bitter pill to swallow
견디기 힘든 고통
be up the creek (without a paddle)
곤경에 처하다
save the bacon
궁지나 위험 등에서 벗어나다

숙어 (ㄱ - ㅅ까지)

공식적

(just) for the record   공식적으로 (그렇다)

공짜

on the house   공짜로, (술집, 회사, 주최 측) 부담으로
fall into laps   거저 먹다
free of charge   무료로 (for nothing, for free, without payment)
for good measure   공짜로

관심

be indifferent to   ~에 무관심하다 (be not interested in, do not care about)
be concerned with   ~에 관심을 갖다 (be interested in)
get something on for   ~에 관심을 가지다
not give somebody the time of the day   ~에게 최소한의 관심도 보이지 않다

구두쇠

penny pincher   구두쇠

구매

be in the market   구매하려 하다

극복

cope with   ~에 대처하다 (treat); ~을 극복하다 (get over, overcome)
get over   ~을 극복하다 (overcome, surmount)
through thick and thin   온갖 어려움을 겪고

근면

eager beaver   일벌레

긍정

look on the bright side   좋은 쪽으로 바라보다

기도

say grace   식전/식후 감사 기도를 드리다

기만

pull[draw] the wool over someone's eyes	(구어) 남의 눈을 속이다 (trick someone by hiding the facts)
take in	~를 속이다 (deceive, delude, cheat)
take someone for a ride	~를 속이다, 비행기 태우다
an old trick	상투적인 수단

긴장

have butterflies in the stomach	매우 긴장하다
on edge	긴장된, 초조한 (nervous, jittery, unrestful, fidgety)
keep on edge	긴장되게 하다, 손에 땀을 쥐게 하다

난처

between a rock and a hard place	이러지도 저러지도 못하고

노력

pull one's socks up	노력해서 발전하다

단속

crack down on	단속하다

당황

drop a brick	당황하게 하다
be at a loss	당황하다, 어찌할 바를 모르다 (be at one's wit's end)
be all at sea	당황하다

독서

read between the lines	행간의 의미를 파악하다, 숨은 의미를 파악하다

마감

meet a deadline	마감일을 맞추다

마음

bring oneself to do	~할 마음이 생기다

말

have a bone to pick (with someone)　(~에게) 따지다, 할 말이 있다

모두

everything but the kitchen sink　　이것저것 몽땅

목숨

have nine lives　　목숨이 아홉 개다

목전

around the corners　　(~날이) 다가오는, 목전인

무시

fly in the face of　　~를 무시하다
thumb one's nose at　　~를 업신여기다
talk down to　　~에게 무시하는 투로 말하다(speak in an impolite manner)
set at naught　　무시하다, 경멸하다(ignore, neglect, not to care about or not fear)
look down on　　~를 깔보다, 내려다보다
turn a deaf ear　　무시하다

미숙

wet behind the ears　　미숙한, 풋내기의(very young and without experience), 철이 덜 든[머리에
피도 안 마른]

born yesterday　　미숙한

밀착

tag along with　　~를 따라다니다

바쁘다

be up to one's ears[neck] in　　~로 정신이 없다, 바쁘다
be tied up　　바쁘다(be busy, have one's hands full)
never a dull moment　　한시도 쉴 틈이 없는

방심

catch someone off guard　　~의 방심을 틈타다

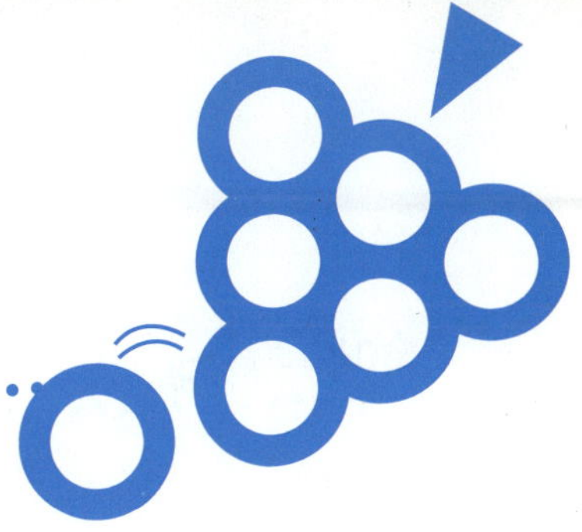

배신

behind someone's back　　　남의 뒤에서

불쾌/불편

be no picnic　　　불편하다

빠르다

like a bat out of hell　　　쏜살같이, 맹속력으로

빡빡하다

packed in like sardines　　　빼곡히 들어찬, (버스 등이) 만원인

사고

accident waiting to happen　　　예고된 사고
fender bender　　　가벼운 접촉 사고

사라지다

do a bunk　　　사라지다

사람

per capita　　　일인당

사로잡다

connected with　　　~에 사로잡힌

생계

keep the pot boiling　　　생계를 꾸려나가다
bring the bacon　　　생계를 꾸려나가다

선호/선택

one's cup of tea　　　~가 좋아하는 타입
have a soft spot for　　　~을 매우 좋아하다
have one's heart set on　　　~을 좋아하다
take a fancy to　　　~을 좋아하다(take to)
take one's pick　　　자신이 원하는 것을 선택하다
Your best bet will be ~　　　너의 최선의 선택은 ~일 것이다

숙어(ㄱ - ㅅ까지)

성공

manage to do   ~하는 데 성공하다

소용

no point of -ing   ~해도 소용없는
What's the point of -ing?   ~하는 게 무슨 소용 있나요?

속도

step on it   속도를 내다

솔직

call a spade a spade   사실대로 말하다, 꾸미지 않고 말하다(be outspoken)
on the square   정직한(honest, on the level); 믿을 만한(trustworthy)
on the level   솔직한; 공평한
speak one's mind   솔직하게 이야기하다(speak frankly)
mean business   진심이다(be serious)
talk turkey   솔직히 말하다
without reserve[reservation]   기탄없이, 솔직하게 *cf.* with reserve 머뭇거리며
wear one's heart (out) on one's sleeve   솔직히 말하다(speak out)
make a clean breast of   ~을 다 털어놓다(speak out)
speak out   솔직히 말하다, 속을 다 털어놓다

순간

in the wink of an eye   눈 깜짝할 사이에, 순간적으로
split second   눈 깜짝할 사이에

술

drink like a fish   술을 물 마시 듯 마시다, 술을 매우 잘 마시다
have rounds for each other   다른 사람들과 술잔을 돌리다

승리

come out on top   이기다, 승리하다
carry the day   승리하다, 이기다
take the cake   이기다, 승리하다
pip someone at the post   ~에게 이기다, 승리하다
sweep the board   완승을 거두다, 압승하다

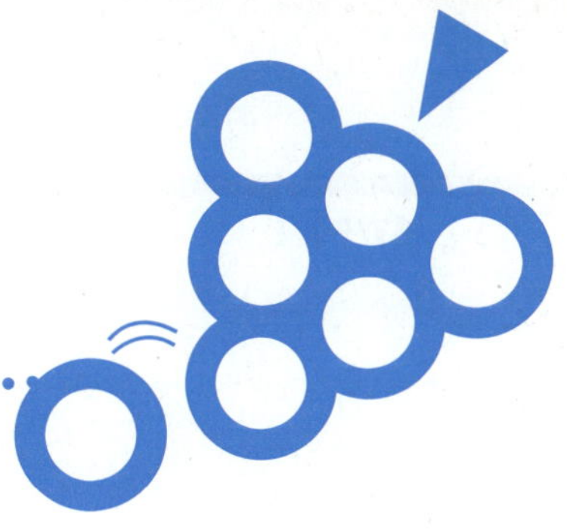

wipe the floor with someone	~를 참패시키다, 크게 이기다

승계
follow in someone's footsteps	~의 대를 잇다

시작
take up	착수하다, 시작하다(begin, commence, launch, start)
enter into	~을 시작하다(commence); ~을 공감하다(sympathize)
set off	출발하다, 시작하다(start, begin a usually long or difficult course of action with a clear purpose)
lead off with	시작하다(start, begin, launch)
turn over a new leaf	새로운 삶을 시작하다(begin a new life)
strike up	(대화를) 시작하다(begin, start, commence)
set in	시작되다
(start) from scratch	아무것도 없는 데서부터, 처음부터 다시 (시작하다)
go back to square one	처음으로 되돌아가다
get the show on the road	(일을) 시작하다
hit the ground running	(새 사업 등의 준비 단계를 끝내고) 본격적으로 시작하다

시중
do the honors	시중들다

신나다
have a field day with something	~하느라 신이 나다

신물
be fed up (with someone or something)	(~에) 질리다, 신물이 나다

실수
go to pot	부주의로 큰 손해를 입다
put one's foot in[into] it[one's mouth]	실수하다(do a wrong thing, make a blunder); 부주의로 곤경에 빠지다(be in hot water by carelessness)
come a cropper	실수하다

실천
practice what one preaches	남에게 설교하는 바를 몸소 실천하다

A. 다음 빈칸에 알맞은 말을 채우세요.

1. I will do it when it comes __________ the crunch.
급해지면 할 거야.

2. I can __________ my socks up in such a short time.
난 단기간에 발전할 수 있어.

3. The ruling party __________ the boards in the general election.
이번 총선에서 여당이 압승을 거두었다.

4. She __________ the door on his proposal of marriage in a seemingly roundabout way.
그녀는 그의 결혼 신청을 겉으로 보기에는 완곡하게(하지만 실제로는 완강히) 거절했다.

B. 다음 우리말에 적절한 어휘를 골라 체크하세요.

5. have ☐ rounds for each other 술잔을 돌리다
　　　☐ glasses

6. do the ☐ services 시중들다
　　　☐ honors

7. have a ☐ field day with something ~하느라 신나다
　　　☐ yard

Answers

1. to
2. pull
3. swept
4. shut
5. rounds
6. honors
7. field

★ Real Test _ 해당 범위 연습문제

Choose the best word for the blank.

1. A: Why is Robert always so argumentative?
   B: I don't know, but it seems he always has a bone to __________ with someone.
   (a) pick
   (b) select
   (c) draw
   (d) choose

2. A: I've invited the Jones to dinner. Do you know whether they drink?
   B: They both drink like a __________, so you'd better be prepared.
   (a) whale
   (b) fish
   (c) drunkard
   (d) sot

3. A: Why should I rent this video?
   B: Because it's so interesting and it will __________ you on the edge of your seat until
      the end.
   (a) keep
   (b) hold
   (c) make
   (d) put

4. A: The stock market has been very unstable. I'm worried because I have invested in
      stocks.
   B: Me, too. I think we should find a way to __________ our bacon.
   (a) eat
   (b) save
   (c) take
   (d) make

5. A: Why did you close down your shop so suddenly?
   B: Because my accountant took me for a __________ and now I'm bankrupt.
   (a) ride
   (b) trip
   (c) shot
   (d) deceive

★**Random Test** _ 모든 범위의 연습문제

Choose the best word for the blank.

6. A: The people in the disco were packed in like __________.
B: There must not have been much room to dance.
(a) multitude
(b) crowd
(c) throng
(d) sardines

7. A: What made you change your lifestyle so suddenly?
B: I was reading this book last month and it really made me __________ the light.
(a) catch
(b) get
(c) see
(d) write

8. A: Why were they out fishing in such a small boat on a windy day?
B: This was an accident waiting to __________.
(a) make
(b) happen
(c) reserve
(d) occur

9. A: Betty, I'm going to turn over a new __________ and get up early every day.
B: I can't wait until tomorrow morning.
(a) resolution
(b) life
(c) mind
(d) leaf

10. A: Can we adapt an old contract and use it in this case?
B: It would be best to start from __________ and make a completely new one.
(a) nothing
(b) scratch
(c) start
(d) injury

11. A: How was the football game last night?

B: It was great. We __________ them.

(a) talked through

(b) rose to the occasion

(c) put on airs

(d) wiped the floor with

12. A: Why did you run away? It was just the sound of an engine backfiring.

B: I thought it was a gun firing and I got the __________ up me.

(a) ride

(b) back

(c) wind

(d) shake

13. A: Why are both the father and the son in the Simpsons almost totally bald?

B: Who knows? Perhaps it __________ the family.

(a) runs in

(b) takes to

(c) makes up

(d) leap out

14. A: He is unable to hear the difference between musical notes.

B: Do you mean he is __________?

(a) sound-proof

(b) sound-deaf

(c) tone-proof

(d) tone-deaf

15. A: He __________ on air these days; his wife is expecting a baby.

B: Is that true? When is the baby due?

(a) jumps

(b) walks

(c) rides

(d) floats

Section Switch

The BMA called on the government to ramp up its anti-smoking drive and introduce legislation to make enclosed public places smoke-free. Women who smoke are twice as likely to be infertile as non-smokers, the report said. Furthermore, smoking is linked to up to 5,000 miscarriages a year and around 1,200 cases of malignant cervical cancer. "Women are generally aware that they should not smoke while pregnant but the message needs to be far stronger," Nathanson told reporters. "Men and women who think they might one day want children should bin cigarettes."

Translation

BMA는 정부에게 금연 운동을 강화하고 실내 공공 공간들을 담배 연기가 없는 지역으로 만드는 법을 도입할 것을 촉구했다. 보고서에 따르면, 담배를 피우는 여성들이 담배를 피우지 않는 여성들보다 불임이 될 가능성이 두 배 더 높다고 한다. 더욱이 흡연은 연간 5,000건에 이르는 유산과 약 1,200건의 악성 경부암과 관련이 있다. "여성들은 대개 임신 중에는 담배를 피우지 말아야 한다는 것을 알고 있지만 그 메시지는 훨씬 더 강력해져야 할 필요가 있습니다." 라고 내이썬손은 기자들에게 말했다. "언젠가 아이를 가지고 싶은 남성이나 여성들은 담배를 끊어야만 합니다."

Vocabulary

call on somebody to do ~에게 …하라고 요구하다

ramp up 적극적으로 추진하다

anti-smoking drive 금연 운동

introduce ~을 도입하다

legislation 입법, 법률 제정

enclosed (공간이 벽이나 어떤 장치물로) 막힌

smoke-free 담배 연기가 없는

infertile 불임의

be linked to ~와 연관되다

miscarriage 유산

malignant 악성의

cervical cancer 경부암

bin ~을 포기하다, 버리다

Chapter 3

숙어(2)

숙어란 단어와 단어의 조합이면서도 연어와는 달리 결합된 단어들이 가지는 일체적 의미가 원래의 뜻과는 크게 다른 뜻으로 변하여 사용되는 것을 말한다고, 앞서 apply the ointment(연고를 바르다)와 bring the bacon(생계를 꾸려나가다)을 예로 들어 설명했다.

Chapter 2에 이어 이러한 숙어 표현을 계속해서 살펴보기로 한다.

A. 다음 중 우리말에 적절한 어휘를 골라 체크하세요.

1. get ☐ straight A's 올 에이를 받다
       ☐ full

2. the baby ☐ complex 출산 우울증
         ☐ blues

3. ☐ whistle in the dark 허세
  ☐ shot

4. ☐ hook off the phone 전화를 끊다
  ☐ get

B. 우리말 의미에 알맞게 빈칸을 채워 표현을 완성하세요.

5. 이해하다   _______ch on to
                fig_______ out

6. 질책하다, 꾸짖다   call on the ca_______t
                     call d_______n

7. 은닉하다, 감추다   cl_______ked in mystery
                     sweep under the r_______g

Answers

1. straight
2. blues
3. whistle
4. get off
5. catch, figure
6. carpet, down
7. cloaked, rug

650 돌파를 위해서 **꼭 외워야 할 숙어**(ㅇ - ㅎ까지)

아부/아첨

butter up	~에게 아부하다(try to get the favor of a person through flattery)
curry favor with	~에게 아첨하다

아프다

under the weather	몸이 아픈

알다

know something backward(s) and forward(s)	~에 대해서 죄다 알다
know something inside out	~에 대해서 죄다 알다
have an eye for	~에 대한 식견이 있다
know the score	잘 알고 있다

애정

have a big crush	반하다

약점

Achilles' heel	취약점

연기

hold over	~을 연기하다(postpone, defer, delay, put off)
take a rain check	(약속 · 초대 등을) 나중으로 미루다
put a hold on	~를 보류하다
put off	~을 연기하다
put something on the back burner	~을 뒤로 미루다
put off evil days	하기 싫은 일을 뒤로 미루다

연락

get hold of	~와 연락하다

완료

go to town (on something)	(~에 대해) 확실히 끝내다

요령

know the ropes	요령을 알다(be experienced, know knack)
learn the ropes	요령을 터득하다(become familiar with)

숙어(ㅇ - ㅎ까지)

get the hang of   ~의 요령을 터득하다

요청
for the asking   달라고 하기만 하면

우수함
cut above everyone   누구보다도 낫다
leave someone standing   ~를 압도하다

우연
accidentally on purpose   우연을 가장해서 고의로

우울
the baby blues   출산 우울증
down in the dumps   침체된, 우울한

울다
cry one's eyes out   눈이 빠지도록 울다

원점
be back to the (old) drawing board   다시 원점으로 돌아오다

위기
close call   위기일발, 아슬아슬한 순간(narrow escape, narrow squeak)
hang by a thread   매우 위태롭다(be in a very uncertain state)
narrow escape   위기일발
touch-and-go   일촉즉발의, 아슬아슬한, 불안한
the blind leading the blind   위험천만한

위로
a blessing in disguise   전화위복

위험
go off the deep end   위험을 무릅쓰다(run a risk); 자제력을 잃다(lose self-restraint)
take the bull by the horns   위험을 무릅쓰다

유용

all the rage
크게 유행하는(very fashionable)

come in handy
유용하다

은닉

cloaked in mystery
은밀하게 감춘

sweep under the rug
감추다

음치

I can't carry a tune
나는 음치이다

tone deaf
음치의

❍ 오답 피하기 tone blind (X) tone disabled (X)

응보

serve someone right
응당 받아야 할 것을 받다

이익

do good
도움이 되다

이해

catch on to
~을 이해하다(understand, learn about)

figure out
~을 이해하다(comprehend, make out)

get across
~을 납득시키다, 이해시키다

get[take, catch] hold of
~을 붙잡다; ~을 이해하다; ~와 연락이 닿다

get the message[picture]
상황을 이해하다(understand the situation)

get the knack[hang] of
~을 이해하다

get a grip on
~을 이해하다(understand, figure out, make out, comprehend)

It's all Greek to me.
금시초문이다, 전혀 이해할 수 없다(It's incomprehensible to me.)

make heads or tails of
(부정문) ~을 이해하다(make sense of)

with all due respect
당신 입장을 이해는 합니다만

익숙

come to terms with
~에 익숙해지다

숙어(ㅇ - ㅎ까지)

인내

pocket one's pride 자존심을 억누르다

  ◎ 오답 피하기 gobble one's pride (X)

swallow one's pride 자존심을 억누르다

일

talk shop (퇴근 후에) 계속 일 이야기를 하다

일상

all in a day's work 일상적인 일

자유

give free rein 맘껏 하게 하다

자제

contain oneself 자제하다

저자세

maintain a low profile 저자세를 취하다

전력

every trick in the book 가능한 모든 수단

전문

right up/down someone's alley 전문 영역

전화

get off the phone 전화를 끊다

점수

do well on the exam 시험에서 선전하다

get a good grade[mark] 좋은 점수를 받다

get straight A's 올 에이를 받다

접대

buy the next round 이번에 한번 사다

정도
get too far   정도가 심하다

정리
get one's act together   마음을 가다듬다

정장
black tie dinner   정장 파티

정확
on the button   정확한(exactly right)
put one's finger on   ~을 꼭 집어 말하다(determine exactly)
smack dab in the middle (of something)   ~의 정면으로, 정확하게

종료
call it a day   하루 일을 끝내다(call it a night, call it quits)
get through with   ~을 끝내다(finish, complete)
go by the board   중단하다
leave for the day   퇴근하다
● 오답 피하기 quit for the day (X) stop for the day (X)
wrap up   ~을 끝내다, 마치다(pack up)
wind up   ~을 끝내다(finish, stop, bring to an end gradually)

죽음
rest in peace   영면하다

준비
save[have] (something) for a rainy day 만약의 사태에 대비하다

즉석/즉시
play it by ear   즉흥 연주를 하다(improvise)
on the spur of the moment   즉석에서(on the spot); 충동적으로(without previous thought)
off hand   즉시(at once, immediately, without time to think or prepare)
in no time   즉시(soon, at once, immediately)
right off the bat   즉시(right away)
No sooner said than done   바로 시행하겠습니다

at the drop of a hat   신호가 있자마자; 곧

증명

call one's bluff   증명하다, 입증하다

지겨움

sick and tired of   ~에 질린, 신물이 난

질책

call on the carpet   ~를 질책하다
call down   ~를 꾸짖다(scold, chide, reproach, reprehend)
be dressed down   꾸지람을 듣다(be taken to task)
jump down someone's throat   호되게 혼내다

참여

take part in   ~에 참여하다

책임

carry the can   책임을 지고 진행하다
Everyone blames everyone else. 서로 책임을 전가하다.
face the music   자진하여 책임을 지다(accept your punishment)
be liable to do   ~하기 쉽다 *cf.* be liable for ~대해 책임이 있다
answer for   ~에 대해 책임을 지다(be responsible for)
pass the buck   책임을 전가하다
play fast and loose   무책임하게 행동하다(act in an irresponsible manner)
in charge of   ~을 담당하고 있는, 책임지고 있는

최고

come off second best   패배하다
second to none   최고의(the best)
take the biscuit   안 좋은 쪽으로 최고이다

최선

bend over backwards   최선을 다해 ~하다
          ex. She bent over backwards to pass the exam. 그녀는 그 시험에 통과하기 위해 최선을 다했다.

최소

the straw that broke the camel's back 최후의 매우 작은 부담

추모

pay one's last respect　　　　　　추모하다

추태

make a scene　　　　　　난리를 부리다, 추태를 부리다

출세

rise through the ranks　　　　　　낮은 신분에서 출세하다

취임

take the mantle of　　　　　　~에 취임하다

칭찬

a pat on the back　　　　　　칭찬, 격려(a gesture of praise or encouragement)

타협/화해

bury the hatchet　　　　　　화해하다
hold out an olive branch　　　　　　화해하다
make up with　　　　　　~와 화해하다

태만

play hooky　　　　　　땡땡이치다

통제

rule the roost　　　　　　통제하다

특별

in particular　　　　　　특별히

파산

go down the tube　　　　　　파산하다

숙어(ㅇ - ㅎ까지)

항복/패배

give in to	~에 굴복하다 *cf.* give in ~을 제출하다
lose the day	패배하다
throw in the towel	패배를 인정하다(admit defeat), 항복하다(surrender)
throw in the sponge	패배를 인정하다(admit defeat), 항복하다(surrender)
eat crow	실수[패배]를 인정하다(admit you are mistaken or defeated), 굴욕을 참다
meet one's Waterloo	패하다(나폴레옹이 전투에서 크게 패한 곳이 Waterloo인데서 유래)

핵심

(have) an ace in the hole	비장의 무기(를 가지다)
hit home	핵심을 찌르다, 정곡을 찌르다
hit the nail on the head	핵심을 찌르다(say exactly the right thing)
go[come] home	급소를 깊이 찌르다, 가슴 깊이 호소하다(be clearly understood by someone, make someone clearly understand something)
boil down to	결국 ~로 (집약)되다(come down to, can be summarized into)
the name of the game	가장 중요한 점, 본질
part and parcel	중요 부분, 요점(integral part)
hit the bull's eye	과녁의 중심을 맞히다; 정곡을 찌르다; 대성공을 거두다
wide of the mark	적절치 못한(irrelevant), 요점에서 벗어난

행운

lady luck	행운의 여신
saved by the bell	운 좋게 곤란을 면하다
take pot luck	기회를 얻다

행복

on cloud nine	매우 행복한, 날아갈 듯이 기쁜(very happy, cheerful)

허무

to no avail	헛되이

허세

whistle in the dark	허세

화

blow a fuse	격분하다

blow off one's steam	격분하다
be in the doghouse	엄청나게 화가 나다
do one's nut	화가 엄청나다
lose one's temper	화를 내다(become angry)
drive someone up the wall	누구를 화나게 하다(drive someone mad)
throw[have] a fit	노발대발하다(become upset, be very angry)
go to pieces	화를 내다
hit the ceiling	화를 내다(become angry)
hit the roof	화를 내다
rub it in	약 올리다, 자꾸 들먹이다
rub someone the wrong way	~를 화나게 하다(annoy someone)
see red	격노하다(become angry, get infuriated)
stir the pot	화나게 하다
blow one's top	매우 화가 나다(hit the ceiling)
fly off the handle	느닷없이 화내다
step on someone's toes	화를 돋우다
go against the grain	화나게 하다

회복

| come full circle | 회복하다 |

회피

| beat around[about] the bush | 돌려서 말하다 |

효과

cut ice	효과가 있다(have effect)
hold good	유효하다(remain valid)
do the trick	효과가 있다

휴식

| get away from it all | 번거로운 일상생활에서 떠나다 |
| rest on your laurels | 푹 쉬다 오다 |

희망

| Tomorrow is another day. | 내일은 내일의 태양이 뜬다, 오늘이 끝이 아니야(그러니까 낙심하지 마라). (영화 《바람과 함께 사라지다》에 등장해 유명해진 말) |

A. 다음 빈칸에 들어갈 적절한 표현을 쓰세요.

1. Everyone just wants to pass the __________ to the next person.

누구나 그저 남에게 책임을 미루기를 바란다.

2. I saw you on TV. But why did you have to take the __________? Are you proud of yourself for doing it?

널 TV에서 봤어. 하지만 왜 안 좋은 예로 나온 거야? 그렇게 한 게 자랑스럽니?

3. Due to a sudden server shut down, I will assume that all the projects now go by the __________.

갑작스럽게 서버가 다운돼 내 예상에 모든 프로젝트들이 다 중단되어 버릴 것이다.

B. 다음 숙어들 중 공통성이 떨어지는 숙어를 고르세요.

4. (a) give in to
(b) lose the day
(c) go to pieces

5. (a) call it a day
(b) get a grip on
(c) get through with

6. (a) carry the can
(b) call on the carpet
(c) be dressed down

Answers
1. buck
2. biscuit
3. board
4. (c)
5. (b)
6. (a)

★ **Real Test** _ 해당 범위 연습문제

Choose the best word for the blank.

1. A: The fire was terrifying!
   B: But it was a blessing in __________ because now people will be more careful with fire.
   (a) pretense
   (b) disguise
   (c) veil
   (d) bad

2. A: Shall I save these old newspapers?
   B: Yeah, they might come in __________ when we clean the windows.
   (a) handy
   (b) helpful
   (c) good
   (d) well

3. A: Stop beating about the __________ and tell me why you can't do it.
   B: Umm... it's because I am not really comfortable with you.
   (a) bush
   (b) shrub
   (c) wood
   (d) forest

4. A: What you said about how our customers respond to ads hit the __________ on the head.
   B: I only said what seemed obvious.
   (a) bolt
   (b) dowel
   (c) punch
   (d) nail

5. When we make mistakes, he brings it to our attention, but he doesn't __________ the handle like he used to.
   (a) blow off
   (b) take off
   (c) fly off
   (d) hang off

★**Random Test** _ 모든 범위의 연습문제

Choose the best word for the blank.

6. A: It looks like we're going back to __________ one on this building plan.
B: It's too bad we can't afford the first plan we made.
(a) same
(b) square
(c) point
(d) green

7. A: Gee, what color necktie do you think I should wear to the ceremony?
B: Don't make a __________ out of a molehill. Any color will be okay.
(a) castle
(b) fortress
(c) mountain
(d) tower

8. A: When the principal retires, it will be hard to __________ his shoes.
B: Yes, he has done a lot for this school.
(a) replace
(b) fill
(c) fulfil
(d) displace

9. A: We need to get Mr. Jones on our side.
B: I agree. He's a force to be __________ with.
(a) neglected
(b) proud
(c) reckoned
(d) understood

10. A: What was the name of that actress in "Casablanca"?
B: Uh... Uh.... Her name is on the tip of my __________, but I can't think of it.
(a) lips
(b) mouth
(c) throat
(d) tongue

11. Lizzy stuffed her mouth full and __________ to get them down with a gulp of water.
    (a) managed
    (b) confiscated
    (c) drained
    (d) lamented

12. Telecommunication __________ such a prominent part in our daily lives that we should do our best to understand its consequences.
    (a) lies
    (b) sets
    (c) plays
    (d) drains

13. You are talking nonsense, Jack. What you have just said is quite __________.
    (a) out of the point
    (b) to the point
    (c) beside the point
    (d) against the point

14. Too bad she missed the train, but it __________ her right for getting up so late this morning.
    (a) makes
    (b) sends
    (c) serves
    (d) puts

15. If you are too strong in your opinions, your comments will definitely __________.
    (a) come full circle
    (b) go down the tube
    (c) lose the day
    (d) stir the pot

Section Switch

Charles Darwin, the author of the influential book The Origin of Species lamented that nobody seemed to understand that natural selection is a process without purpose, that is, without a preordained outcome and without an active selection process as in 'Man's selection.'

Translation

〈종의 기원〉이라는 영향력 있는 책의 저자인 찰스 다윈은 자연 선택이 우연한 과정, 즉 어떤 운명적으로 예정된 결과나 '인간의 선택' 에서와 같은 적극적인 선택 과정이 없는 과정이라는 것을 이해하는 사람이 아무도 없는 것 같다면서 개탄했다.

Vocabulary

influential 영향력 있는
lament 개탄하다
natural selection 자연 선택
process 과정
that is 즉, 다시 말해
without purpose 의도하지 않고, 우연히
preordained (운명이) 이미 정해져 있는, 필연적인
outcome 결과

Chapter 4

혼동되는단어

TEPS에서 출제되는 어휘 문제는 일반적인 영어 시험과는 다르다. 즉, 하나의 단어가 가지는 다양한 의미를 물어본다든지 아니면 형태가 비슷하거나 의미가 유사하지만 분명히 다른 뜻을 가지고 있는 어휘들을 물어보는 것이 보편적이다.

따라서 이 책에서는 단어의 기본적인 뜻뿐 아니라, 다양한 뜻 그리고 혼동되는 철자와 의미에 주목해서 공부할 수 있게 정리했다.

이번 Chapter에서는 이러한 혼동 어휘들을 한데 모아 정리해보도록 한다.

A. 다음은 철자가 혼동되는 단어들. 빈칸에 해당되는 단어의 뜻을 써보세요.

1. adverse   ____________
    advert   유의하다, 논급하다
    averse   싫어하는, ~에 반대하는

2. affinity   좋아함
    infinity   ____________

3. avoid   ~을 피하다
    ovoid   ____________

4. complement   ____________
    compliment   칭찬, 치하, 경의
    implement   이행하다, 권한을 주다

5. corpulent   뚱뚱한
    opulent   ____________

B. 다음 단어의 빈칸에 TEPS에서 잘 나오는 다른 뜻을 써보세요.

6. amenity   ① 편리성
    ② ____________

7. arbitrary   ① 임의적인
    ② ____________

8. betray   ① 배신하다
    ② ____________

9. momentum   ① 운동량, 힘
    ② ____________

Answers

1. 불리한, 해로운
2. 무한
3. 계란형의
4. 보충하다
5. 풍부한
6. 예절
7. 독단적인
8. 드러내다
9. 추진력

1차적인 의미 외에 2차적인 의미도 제대로 알아두어야 하는 단어

abandon
① 포기하다
② 다루지 않다

affect
① 영향을 끼치다
② 피해를 끼치다 *ex.* affected area 피해 입은 지역

arbitrary
① 임의적인
② 독단적인

amenity
① 편리성
② 예절

betray
① 배신하다
② 드러내다

bulb
① 전구
② 구근 식물

caliber
① (총포의) 구경
② 우수성

chair
① 의자
② 회의를 주재하다

challenge
① 도전하다
② 반박하다

charter
① 헌장
② 전세 내다

dismiss
① 해고하다
② 소송을 기각하다

divulge	① 누설하다 ② 알리다
enmesh	① 빠뜨리다 ② 그물에 걸리게 하다
exit	① 탈출하다 ② 내리다, 나가다
momentum	① 운동량, 힘 ② 추진력

STEP 2 Word Clinic

철자가 혼동되는 단어

able	유능한
liable	의무가 있는
abundant	풍부한
redundant	장황한
accede	응하다, 동의하다; 취임하다
concede	인정하다, 승인하다
access	v. 접근하다 n. 접근
excess	과도, 과잉
adolescent	사춘기의 *cf.* 명사형은 adolescense
convalescent	회복기의
adverse	불리한, 해로운
advert	유의하다, 논급하다
averse	싫어하는, ~에 반대하는
affinity	좋아함
infinity	무한
affect	~에 영향을 미치다, 작용하다
affectation	잘난 척하기, 꾸밈, 꾸미는 태도
affectionate	애정이 있는, 애정이 넘치는
affection	사랑, 애정
effect	영향
afflux	유입
efflux	(액체, 공기 등의) 유출
aggression	침략, 침범
egression	퇴출

airless	공기가 없는
hairless	털이 없는
heirless	상속인이 없는
allay	가라앉히다
alley	골목, 소로
ally	동맹하다, 연맹하다
alloy	합금
rally	다시 모으다, 다시 모이다
allude	① 암시하다, 넌지시 비치다
	② 언급하다
elude	피하다
allure	꾀다, 유혹하다
lure	유혹하다
allusion	암시, 언급
delusion	망상
illusion	환상
amend	수정하다, 개정하다
amends	보상, 배상
emend	(책을) 교정하다
mend	고치다, 수선하다
anticipate	예상하다
participate	참가하다
apathetic	무관심한, 냉담한
pathetic	애처로운
apprehend	이해하다
comprehend	포함하다; 이해하다

appropriate	적절한, 적당한
approximate	접근하다
proxy	대리, 위임장
arithmetic	산수
mathematics	수학
arouse	깨우다
arise	발생하다
rouse	잠에서 깨우다, 분기하다
ascetic	금욕생활의
aseptic	무균의
(a)esthetic	미학적인
ecstatic	무아지경의
avocation	부업, 취미
evocation	불러일으킴
vocation	본업, 천직
vacation	휴가
avoid	~을 피하다
ovoid	계란형의
avow	인정하다, 자백하다
vow	맹세, 서약
bazaar	(자선기금 등이 목적인) 바자회
bizarre	n. 기괴한 풍경 a. 기괴한
believe	믿다
relieve	① 완화하다
	② 구원하다
biannual	연 2회의
biennial	2년마다의
semiannual	반년마다의

철자가 혼동되는 단어

blush	얼굴을 붉히다
flash	번쩍이다, 번쩍거리다
flush	① 변기의 물을 내리다
	② 붉어지다
boisterous	떠들썩한
bolster	강화하다, 보강하다
cessation	정지
session	(의회 등의) 개회
chimp	침팬지
shrimp	새우
cite	인용하다, 인증하다
incite	자극하다
site	부지, 위치
clandestine	비밀스러운
destine	운명
claw	(고양이, 매 등의) 발톱
flaw	결함, 결점
cluster	(과실, 꽃 등의) 한 송이, 한 덩어리
fluster	혼란케 하다
command	① 경치를 바라보다
	② 명령하다
commence	시작하다
commend	맡기다, 칭찬하다
commendation	칭찬, 추천
commendment	명령, 지령
comment	논평, 비평

complement	보충하다
compliment	칭찬, 치하, 경의
implement	이행하다, 권한을 주다
conclusive	결정적인
exclusive	배타적인
inclusive	포함하는
reclusive	은둔적인
secluded	은둔하는
connote	내포하다
denote	뜻하다
corpulent	뚱뚱한
opulent	풍부한
cur	잡종 개, 비열한 사람
concur	동의하다, 동시에 일어나다
incur	초래하다
occur	발생하다, (생각 등이) 떠오르다
recur	재발하다
flea	벼룩
flee	도망치다, 달아나다
fleece	바가지 씌우다, 속임수로 빼앗다
fleet	① 함대, 선단
	② v. 움직이다 a. 빠른

A. 다음 문장의 의미에 맞게 밑줄 친 단어의 2차적인 의미를 써보세요.

1. Everybody in my class is not willing to follow his <u>arbitrary</u> action.
우리 반의 누구도 그의 독단적인 행동을 따르려 하지 않는다. ___________________

2. The chairman <u>challenged</u> the result of the audit last night.
회장은 어젯밤 감사의 결과에 대하여 반박했다. ___________________

3. He was renowned for his ceaseless <u>momentum</u> at once.
그는 한때 거침없는 추진력으로 명성을 날렸었다. ___________________

B. 다음 중 우리말에 적절한 어휘를 골라 체크하세요.

4. The period of ☐ adolescence 사춘기
☐ convalescent

5. ☐ incite an axiom 경구를 인용하다
☐ cite

6. ☐ compliment an operation 작전을 수행하다
☐ implement

C. 다음 표현의 우리말 의미를 완성하세요.

7. chair the meeting　　　회의를 ___________ 하다

8. charter bus　　　___________ 버스

9. flea market　　　___________ 시장

Answers
1. 독단적인
2. 반박하다
3. 추진력
4. adolescence
5. cite
6. implement
7. 주재
8. 전세
9. 벼룩

★ Real Test _ 해당 범위 연습문제

Choose the best word for the blank.

1. A: Could you tell me where Brown & Cordon's is?
   B: If you __________ this elevator on the sixth floor, you can see the reception.
   (a) exit
   (b) enter
   (c) escape
   (d) go

2. You must __________ enough about your career to convince the HR department that you are the right person for that job.
   (a) divulge
   (b) delude
   (c) describe
   (d) decry

3. Their __________ marriage took place in an alienated local church last week.
   (a) gorgeous
   (b) clandestine
   (c) tediously long
   (d) scandalous

4. The officer's claim in the military court was __________ due to insufficient evidence.
   (a) dismissed
   (b) charged
   (c) accepted
   (d) dismissed

5. The children were so excited about their vacation trip that they became __________ and had to be calmed down.
   (a) lanky
   (b) staid
   (c) boisterous
   (d) forthright

★Random Test _ 모든 범위의 연습문제

Choose the best word for the blank.

6. A: I regret paying ___________ for this stuff.
B: You've been ripped off.
(a) highly
(b) dearly
(c) mainly
(d) sincerely

7. A good way of ridding yourself of certain kinds of ___________ is to become aware of opinion held in social circles different from your own.
(a) dogmatism
(b) positivism
(c) conservatism
(d) liberalism

8. From the moment he set up the denounced shop on Avenue K, Stanley Kaplan was a ___________ in the educational world.
(a) pariah
(b) novice
(c) ex-convict
(d) patriot

9. When Sally tries to do her arithmetic problems, she uses her eraser as often as her pencil, because she makes so many ___________.
(a) numbers
(b) mistakes
(c) answers
(d) problems

10. They ___________ the meeting as best they could.
(a) lauded
(b) publicized
(c) launched
(d) ignored

11. The doctor gave the prescription to him and fortunately his pain __________ during the night.
(a) subsided
(b) soared
(c) appeared
(d) exposed

12. Geologists have discovered 1.43 billion-year-old fossils of deep-sea microbes, providing more evidence that life may have __________ on the bottom of the ocean
(a) originated
(b) created
(c) suggested
(d) disclosed

13. The updated information is sent in __________ of computer code on FM radio frequencies, sometimes sharing wavelengths with radio programs.
(a) packets
(b) pieces
(c) classes
(d) bundles

14. African states with Atlantic coastlines will use satellite surveillance to curb __________ of fish which robs them of more than half their potential annual catch.
(a) hunting
(b) shooting
(c) poaching
(d) catching

15. Rainstorms have __________ launch preparations but there was an 80 percent chance of good weather for Saturday.
(a) helped
(b) assisted
(c) plagued
(d) missed

Section Switch

Great cities have been built with no regard of us. The shape and dimensions of the skyscrapers depend entirely on the necessity of obtaining maximum income per square foot of ground. This caused the construction of gigantic buildings where too large masses of human beings are crowded together.

Translation

대도시는 우리를 전혀 고려하지 않은 채 만들어졌다. 초고층 건물들의 모양과 크기는 전적으로 1평방피트 단위 면적당 최대한의 수입을 올리기 위한 필요성에 따라 결정되는 것이다. 이로 인해 지나치게 많은 사람들로 빽빽하게 들어차 있는 거대한 건물들을 짓게 되었다.

Vocabulary

with no regard of ~를 고려하지 않고
shape 모양
dimension 크기
skyscraper 초고층 건물
depend on ~에 따라 좌지우지되다
necessity 필요성
obtain ~을 얻다, 획득하다
maximum income 최대 수입
square foot 평방피트
(too large) masses of (지나치게) 많은
be crowded 바글바글하다

2어 동사

2어 동사란 하나의 중심 동사를 기준으로 다양한 전치사와 부사가 결합되어 쓰이는 동사구를 말한다. 각 동사구의 의미를 헷갈리지 않도록 주의해서 익혀두도록 한다.

A. 우리말에 맞는 어휘를 골라 체크하세요.

1. ☐ bargain in 불쑥 찾아들다
☐ barge

2. ☐ chip in 기부하다, 제 몫을 내다
☐ choke

3. ☐ pass up 기회를 놓치다
☐ go

B. 다음 문장에 어울리는 어휘를 고르세요.

4. Getting wet in the rain yesterday brought (on / up) my cold.
비오는 날, 비에 젖었기 때문에 감기에 걸렸다.

5. He eased (on / off) the workload of his employees by hiring more staff.
그는 직원을 더 고용하여 직원들의 업무 부담을 줄여주었다.

6. Marriage is all about hammering (out / up) differences between two people.
결혼에서 가장 중요한 것은 서로 다른 두 사람 사이의 절충과 타협이다.

7. Before making an investment you should mull (through / over) it.
투자를 하기에 앞서서 시간을 갖고 신중하게 생각해봐야 한다.

8. Hey, guys, pack it (up / on), it's already 4 o'clock in the morning.
자, 다들 하던 일을 마무리해라, 벌써 새벽 4시라고.

9. After two hours of pursuit, the police finally rounded him (down / up).
2시간의 추격 끝에 경찰은 그를 미침내 체포할 수 있었다.

10. I tried to work (off / with) fat around stomach by exercising.
난 운동을 통해서 내 뱃살을 빼보려고 시도했다.

Answers
1. barge
2. chip
3. pass
4. on
5. off
6. out
7. over
8. up
9. up
10. off

650 돌파를 위해서 꼭 외워야 할 2어 동사(A - Z)

act up	짓궂은 행동으로 장난을 치다
add up	이치에 맞다
back down	물러나다
bank on	의존하다
bargain for	협상하다
barge in	불쑥 찾아 들어가다
bear out	증명하다
beef up	강화하다
boil down	요약되다, 핵심이 되다
boss around	이래라 저래라 하다
bring about	일으키다
bring on	불러오다
bring up	(감기 등을) 일으키다
brush up[on]	상기하다
bump into	우연히 만나다
bump off	죽이다
bundle up	따뜻하게 몸을 감싸다

❍ 오답 피하기 | buckle up (X) bunch up (X)

burn (oneself) out	무리를 하다
call for	① 요구하다 ② (수동태로 써서) 어떤 말을 들어서 마땅하다

care for	좋다

○ **오답 피하기** 그냥 care라고 쓰지 않도록 조심

carry off	이기다, 성공하다
cash in on	돈을 벌다
catch on	유행하다
change down	기어를 내리다
chew over	곰곰이 생각하다
chip in	기부하다, 제 몫을 내다
choke off	가로 막다, 방해하다
chuck up	취소하다
clamp down on	제재하다
cook up	꾸미다; 고안하다
count out	제외하다
count toward	취급되다
crack up	크게 웃게 만들다
crop up	(예상치 못한 일이) 생기다
cry off	취소하다
cut through	중간을 지나가다
dash off	빨리 일을 처리하다

dawn on	생각이 나다
depend on	~에 의지하다, ~에 따라 좌지우지되다
do up	① 수리하다, 고치다 ② 닫다, 조이다
dream up	만들어내다
drop off	데려다놓다
dwell on	염두에 두다

◐ 오답 피하기 think on (X)

ease off	경감되다, 줄어들다
ease up	풀다(relax)
eat at	괴롭히다

◐ 오답 피하기 bug at (X) interrupt at (X)

eat into	잠식하다
egg on	부추기다
end up	결국 ~이 되다
fall off	(신발이) 벗겨지다
fall through	실패하다
figure out	이해하다
fill in	설명하다
fill in for	채워넣다, 대체하다
fix on	결정하다
fix up	설치하다; 수리[수선]하다
fly off	화를 내다

focus on	집중하다
give away	배포하다
give off	발산하다
go out	외출하다, 꺼지다
go for	~을 좋아하다, 들어맞다
go in for	찬성하다
go into	~에 종사하다
go cold turkey	담배, 술을 당장 끊다
go cruising	운전하다
go with	어울리다
goof up	망치다
hammer out	다듬다
hang back	기다리다
hang on	잠깐 기다리다
hang out (with)	(~와) 같이 어울리다
have on	옷을 입다
have over	초대하다
head off	따돌리다
hinge on	달려있다
hold off	잡아두다
hold over	연기하다
hold up	지연시키다; 노상에서 강탈하다
impose on	악용하다
keel over	넘어지다

key(ed) up	긴장하여
knock off	일을 그만두다
lap up	인정하다
lay down	규정하다
lay off	① 해고하다 ② 음식 등을 피하다
lay on	(음식 등을) 준비하다
let down	실망시키다
let off	용서하다
let on	누설하다
let up	(비나 눈이) 멈추다
lock down	(주로 수동태로) 갇혀 있다
lock out of	(수동태로) 열쇠를 두고 잠그다
look into	자세히 조사하다
look over	자세히 들여다보다
look up	찾아보다
look up to	존경하다
lose out	불리해지다
make off	달아나다
muck up	망치다
mull over	신중하게 생각하다
muscle in on	침범하다
open up	열다, 털어놓다, 지사를 열다

opt out	선택하지 않다, 배제하다
own up	인정하다
pack (it) up	마무리하다
pass on	전달하다
pass up	기회를 놓치다
pick up	고르다; 차에 태우다
pin down	의도 따위를 말하게 하다, 정확하게 파악하다
play along	찬성하는 척하다
play up	문제를 일으키다
point out	지적하다
press on	계속하다
psyche out	자신감을 꺾다
pull off	달성하다
rake in	돈을 긁어모으다
rake up	공개하다
rattle off	말을 빨리하다
reck on	기대하다
reel off	읊조리다
resort to	의존하다
ring up	전화하다, 계산하다

round off	만족스럽게 끝나다
round up	체포하다(arrest, apprehend); 모으다
rub in	반복해서 말하다
run into	우연히 만나다
sew up	마무리 짓다
ship out	그만두다 *cf.* **Shape up or ship out.** 제대로 하든지 아니면 그만두어라.
show up	나타나다
sit out	아무 역할도 하지 못하다
sit through	~가 끝날 때까지 가만히 있다
skim through	~을 대충 훑어보다
sleep off	회복하다
sleep on	곰곰이 생각하다
slip up	실수를 하다
snap up	주저 없이 획득하다
split up	결별하다
stamp out	이겨내다
stand down	긴장을 풀고 쉬다
steer away	조심스럽게 빗겨나가다
stick with	~을 고수하다
stir up	자극하다

straighten out   바로 세우다

talk into   ~하게끔 설득하다(persuade는 그냥 to)
talk out of   못하게 만들다

tell on   일러바치다

throw away   버리다

tie(d) up   바쁘다

tighten up   강화하다

tip off   누설하다

touch off   발생시키다

trip up   발생시키다

turn into   변하다

walk out   일을 팽개치다

wind down   진정하다
wind up   결말짓다

wipe out   죽여 버리다; 죽다
➲ 오답 피하기| pass away와 헷갈리게 나온다.

work off   노력으로 제거하다
work out   셈하다, 효력을 발하다
work up   자극하다

wrap things up   마무리하다

write off	감가상각하다
yell at	화를 내다

A. 우리말 의미에 알맞게 빈칸을 채워 표현을 완성하세요.

1. Eric's teacher called me yesterday, because Eric st______s up other children regularly at school.

Eric의 선생님이 어제 내게 전화를 해서 Eric이 학교에서 정기적으로 다른 아이들을 자극시킨다고 말했어요.

2. I missed the class because something cr______ed up.

뭔가 예상치 못했던 일이 생겨서 수업에 빠졌다.

3. She ca______ed off the project, even with the negative situation.

불리한 상황에도 불구하고 그녀는 프로젝트를 성공시켰다.

B. 다음 문장에 이어질 알맞은 표현을 (a) ~ (f) 중 고르세요.

4. Stop playing
5. After the scouts returned, the general pinned
6. The soldiers standed
7. Don't stop and keep pressing
8. Susie has no friends, because she always tells
9. I am putting in all my energy to straighten

> (a) out this company.
> (b) on us to the teacher.
> (c) on, then you will achieve your goal.
> (d) down after 1 week of ambush duty.
> (e) up, I am sick of looking after you.
> (f) down the location of the enemy camp.

4. 문제 좀 그만 일으켜라, 난 이제 네 뒤치다꺼리 해주는 것에 지쳤다.
5. 정찰병이 돌아오자 장군은 적진이 어딘지를 정확하게 파악했다.
6. 병사들은 1주일간의 매복 근무 후에 긴장을 풀고 쉬었다.
7. 포기하지 말고 계속 하다보면 언젠가 너의 목표에 도달할 수 있을 것이다.
8. Susie는 항상 선생님에게 우리에 대해서 일러바치기 때문에 친구가 없다.
9. 난 회사를 바로잡기 위해서 내 모든 에너지를 다 바치고 있다.

Answers

1. stirs
2. cropped
3. carried
4. (e)
5. (f)
6. (d)
7. (c)
8. (b)
9. (a)

★ Real Test _ 해당 범위 연습문제

Choose the best word for the blank.

1. The verdict could __________ on the motives, loyalty and competence of a slate of expert witnesses with divergent opinions.
   (a) decide
   (b) make
   (c) hinge
   (d) hang

2. A: I'm leaving. Are you going to stay a while longer?
   B: Yes, I want to ________ things up here before I quit for the day. See you tomorrow.
   (a) wrap
   (b) finish
   (c) do
   (d) complete

3. A: The weekend ski trip will cost $450 per person.
   B: Wow! __________ me out. I don't have that much money.
   (a) Count
   (b) Erase
   (c) Include
   (d) Regard

4. The result is that consumers pay higher fuel prices while the oil companies __________ an estimated $3 billion in U. S. income taxes.
   (a) take off
   (b) write off
   (c) ride off
   (d) sleep off

5. Despite the opposition of the ruling party, government refuses to __________ down over tax issue.
   (a) back
   (b) clean
   (c) boil
   (d) bring

★**Random Test** _ 모든 범위의 연습문제

Choose the best word for the blank.

6. A: Oh, no. Only 3 days until our midterm exam. And I can't remember anything.
B: Don't worry, I will help you __________ up your memory.
(a) brush
(b) bring
(c) revise
(d) back

7. A: Why did you talk back to your boss?
B: Because, my colleagues __________ me on.
(a) cheered
(b) took
(c) egged
(d) filled

8. A: What's up with your broken arm?
B: I was __________ while riding a bicycle yesterday.
(a) knocked off
(b) keeled over
(c) took off
(d) fall apart

9. Looting __________ at scattered sites around the city, and several foreign embassies began to evacuate nonessential employees and dependents.
(a) abided by
(b) broke out
(c) brought up
(d) resulted in

10. We are __________ Motor Cara Model EC-331, and are pleased to place the following order with you.
(a) in the market for
(b) indifferent to
(c) around the corners
(d) up to our ears in

11. The purpose of the United Nations, as __________ in its Charter, is to maintain world peace and security.
(a) dawn on
(b) laid down
(c) gained on
(d) worked out

12. When I first got to teach this class, so many of the students were lacking confidence and motivation, therefore I am trying to __________ the students.
(a) suit up
(b) get over
(c) straighten out
(d) take over

13. I used to be an overconfident guy. But my girlfriend left me recently. She has really __________ me __________ because ever since I have lost all of my confidence.
(a) psyched - out
(b) took - out
(c) burn - out
(d) worn - out

14. It would be a good idea to __________ the business further before you invest all your money into it.
(a) take hold of
(b) decide on
(c) get through
(d) look into

15. He spoke so quickly that it was difficult to __________ what he was saying.
(a) put forward
(b) take down
(c) follow up
(d) hand in

Section Switch 

No study to the United States would be complete without a discussion of immigrants because America is a nation of immigrants. Since 1607, when the first English settlers reached the New World, over 45 million people have migrated to the United States. This represents the largest migration of people in all of recorded history.

Translation

미국은 이민자들의 나라이기 때문에 미국에 관한 어떤 연구도 이민자들에 대한 논의를 배제하고는 완전할 수 없을 것이다. 최초의 영국 정착민들이 신세계에 도착했던 1607년 이래 4천 5백만 명이 넘는 사람들이 미국으로 이주했다. 이는 역사상 가장 큰 인구 이동을 보여준다.

Vocabulary

study 연구
immigrant 이민자
settler 정착민
migrate 이주하다
represent ~를 나타내다, 보여주다
migration (인구의) 대이동
recorded 기록된

Chapter 6

표현

표현(expression)은 다양한 정의가 가능하다. 여기에서는 숙어와 이디엄에 가깝지만 하나의 대화에서 독립적인 문장으로 쓰이는 것들을 중심으로 다뤄보겠다. 그러니 여러분들도 그러한 체계에서 표현을 정의내리고 접근하길 바란다.

A. 우리말에 맞는 적절한 어휘를 골라 체크하세요.

1. I'm much ☐ obliged. 무척 감사드려요.
　　　　　☐ appreciated.

2. ☐ Keep it up. 계속 그렇게 해.
　　☐ Go

3. I don't ☐ object at all. 나는 전혀 개의치 않아요.
　　　　☐ mind

4. Sample is ☐ ample. 지겨워졌어.
　　　　　☐ adequate.

5. What are you in the ☐ attitude for? 뭘 좋아하세요?
　　　　　　　　　☐ mood

B. 우리말 의미에 알맞게 빈칸을 채워 표현을 완성하세요.

6. 건배합시다.　　　　　I'll dr_____k to that.
　　　　　　　　　　Let's have a to_____t.

7. 긁어 부스럼 만들지 마.　If it ain't broke, don't f_____ it.
　　　　　　　　　　Leave well enough a_____ne.

8. 시간이 잘 간다.　　　Time fl_____s.
　　　　　　　　　Time passes in a fl_____h.

9. 전혀 모르겠어.　　　I haven't a cl_____e.
　　　　　　　　　I haven't the fa_____est idea.

650 돌파를 위해서 꼭 외워야 할 표현

감사

I'm much obliged.	무척 감사드려요.

> ● 오답 피하기 I'm much appreciated/thanked/gratified. (X)

I owe you big.	무척 감사드려요.
It's the thought that counts.	생각만으로도 고맙다.
Thank you for the offer.	제의에 감사드립니다.
Thank you for reminding me.	알려줘서 고마워.
You're a life saver.	정말 많은 도움이 되었어요.

> ● 오답 피하기 You're a benefit saver. (X)

걱정/관심(안심)

Bless you!	① 신의 축복이 있기를 바랍니다.
	② (상대가 재채기 했을 때) 신의 가호가 있기를!
Don't sweat it.	걱정하지 마.
Thanks for asking.	물어봐줘서 고마워.
I couldn't care less.	별로 신경 쓰지 않아.
I can't simply put worries to rest.	걱정을 떨쳐버릴 수가 없어.

건배

I'll drink to that.	건배합시다.
Let's have a toast.	건배합시다.

격려

Keep it up.	계속 그렇게 해.

> ● 오답 피하기 Go it up. (X)

Way to go.	잘했어.

결국

in the long run	결국에는

결론

(to) make a long story short	짧게 줄여 말하자면

계산

Let me take care of dinner.	저녁은 제가 계산하겠습니다.

공평
Fair enough? — 공평하지?

괜찮아
Don't mention it. — (감사 인사나 사과의 말에 대해) 괜찮아, 천만에.

권유
Be my guest. — 당신 먼저 하세요.; 얼마든지요.

권태
Sample is ample. — 지겨워졌어.

그림
A picture is worth a thousand words. — 여러 말보다는 하나의 사진이 더 가치가 있다.

기대
Don't get your hopes up. — 너무 기대하지 마.

기쁨
can't contain oneself — 어쩔 줄을 모르다

기억
Does it ring a bell? — 기억나니?
If my memory serves me right — 내 기억이 맞는다면

기타
what have you — 기타 등등

긴장
Hang in there! — 너무 초조해 마라! (= 참고 견뎌라!)

난항
Do I have a choice? — 달리 방법이 있겠어?

노력
No pain, no gain. — 수고 없이 맺는 열매는 없다.

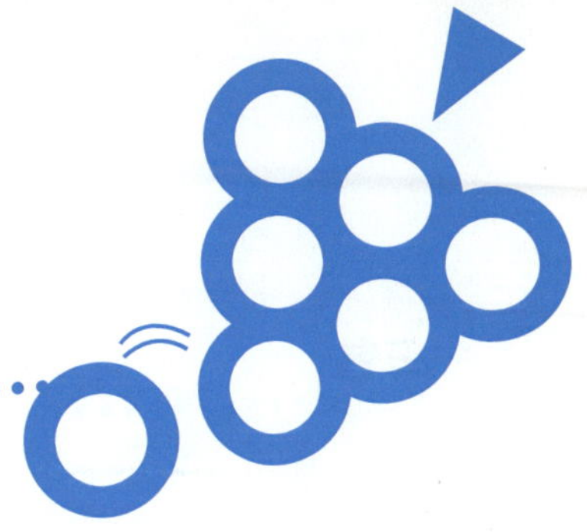

Practice makes perfect. 연습을 하면 완벽해진다.
all the more reason for doing something 그러니까 더욱 ~해야지

다행
Better late than never. 아예 하지 않는 것보단 늦게라도 하는 것이 낫다.

단념
quit while one is (still) ahead (아직) 잘 나갈 때 그만두다
Forget it. 신경 꺼.

당부
Be prepared. 준비 잘해.

대충
That's about it. 대충 그래.

대화
Can I have a word with you? 잠시 이야기 나눌 수 있을까요?
○ 오답 피하기 Can I have a saying with you? (X)

대가
What's it worth? 대가가 뭔데?, 그러면 뭐 해줄 건데?

도발
(Go ahead and) Make my day! 덤빌 테면 덤벼봐!

도움
I'm at your service. 말씀만 하세요.
○ 오답 피하기 I'm at aid/help/assistance. (X)
Two heads are better than one. 백짓장도 맞들면 낫다.

돈
Easy come, easy go. 쉽게 번 돈은 쉽게 써버린다.
Money doesn't grow on trees. 땅 파면 돈 나오냐?!

표현

동의

Consider it done.	물론이지.

○ 오답 피하기 Regard/Think/Take it done. (X)

I will drink to that.	찬성이야.
I will go along with it.	나는 찬성이야.
It's a deal.	찬성이야.
It works for me.	저한테는 맞는 것 같아요.
We have a deal.	그럼 찬성한 거예요.
Deal!	찬성!
Join the club!	나도 마찬가지야!
Now you're talking!	내 말이 그 말이야!
That goes without saying.	(말할 것도 없이) 정말 그렇다.
You bet!	당연하지!
You took the words (right) out of my mouth.	내 말이 바로 그거야.
You can say that again. / You said it!	두말 하면 잔소리지!
just what the doctor ordered	(바로) 필요한 것, (바로) 갖고 싶었던 것
(That's) Fair enough!	(제안에 대하여) 됐어!
Welcome to the club.	나도 그래.
Well said.	지당하십니다.
That's one possibility.	그것도 한 방법이네요.

만일

just in case	만일의 경우

만족

You can't please everyone.	모든 사람들을 만족시킬 수는 없다.

말

One's bark is worse than one's bite.	말은 거칠지만 본성은 그렇게 나쁘지 않다.
Talk is cheap.	말이야 쉽지.

망각

Forgive and forget.	깨끗이 잊어버려.

메시지

Can you take a message?	메시지를 전해주시겠습니까?

○ 오답 피하기 Can you receive a message? (X)

Should I take a message? 메시지를 남기시겠습니까?

◐ 오답 피하기 Should I make/leave/send a message? (X)

무방

Damned if you do, damned if you don't. 해도 안 좋고, 안 해도 안 좋다.
(There's) No harm in trying. 시도하는 거야 괜찮지.
No harm done. 전원 무사함.; 이상 없음.
Whatever turns you on. 아무렴 어때.
I don't mind at all. 나는 전혀 개의치 않아요.

◐ 오답 피하기 I don't object at all. (X)

It can't hurt to ask. 묻는 거야 괜찮겠지.
Take it or leave it. 사든지 말든지.

무시

(go) in one ear and out the other 한 귀로 듣고 한 귀로 흘려버리다

무지

I haven't a clue. 전혀 모르겠어.
I haven't the faintest idea. 전혀 모르겠어.
not know whether one is coming or going 뭐가 뭔지 전혀 모르다
That's news to me. 처음 듣는 소식이다.
(There's) No way to tell. 아무도 모른다.
Your guess is as good as mine. 나도 너처럼 몰라.
You got me there. ① 나도 몰라요. ② 그렇네요.
You've got me there. 모르겠어.

무한

So much for that. / So much for something. 그건 이만 하자.

문의

It never hurts to ask. 그냥 한번 물어봐.

믿다

That'll be the day! 믿을 수가 없어!

표현

바쁘다
I've been keeping busy.　　그동안 바빴어.

반갑다
Fancy meeting you here!　　너를 여기에서 만나게 되다니!
　○ 오답 피하기 Imagine meeting you here! (X)

반박
You wanna bet?　　내기 할래?

발견
You can't miss it.　　쉽게 찾으실 거예요.

배고픔
I'm starving.　　배고파 죽겠다.

보류
cross that bridge when one comes to it　그 때가서 생각하다

보이다
Does it show?　　그래 보이니?

보통
That's just typical.　　그들은 항상 그래.

봉사
First come, first served.　　먼저 오신 분부터 차례대로 제공됩니다.
(Just) Say the word.　　분부만 내리세요.

부스럼
If it ain't broke, don't fix it.　　괜히 긁어 부스럼 만들지 마.
Leave well enough alone.　　긁어 부스럼 만들지 마.

부정
Easier said than done.　　말이 쉽지 (행동하는 건 어려워).
Not in my book.　　나는 그렇게 안 해.

Not that I know of.
내가 아는 한은 그렇지 않아요.

● 오답 피하기 Not that I think of. (X)

No kidding!!
설마 그럴 리가!

● 오답 피하기 No joking!! (X)

부탁

While you are at it
그거 하는 김에

● 오답 피하기 While 부분을 바꿔서 출제함에 조심

불평

The squeaky[squeaking] wheel gets the grease.
우는 아이에게 젖 준다.

Stop whimpering!
우는 소리 좀 그만 해!

Stop whining!
징징 대지마!

비난

Look who's talking.
사돈 남 말하네.

사과

Apology taken.
사과를 받아들일게.

상황

How did everything go?
어떻게 되었나요?

● 오답 피하기 How did everything pass/turn? (X)

서빙

I'll be right back with that.
금방 가지고 돌아오겠습니다.

선택/선호

when push comes to shove
선택의 여지가 없을 때에는

To each his/her own
각자 좋아하는 게 있다

What are you in the mood for?
뭘 좋아하세요?, 뭘 하고 싶으세요?

● 오답 피하기 What are you in the attitude for? (X)

설상가상

add insult to injury
설상가상으로

표현

성공

The third time's the charm. — 세 번째는 성공할 거야.

소개

Let me introduce ~ — ~를 소개해 드리겠습니다

Allow me to introduce ~ — ~를 소개해도 되겠습니까?

오답 피하기 Take/Pardon me to introduce ~ (X)

소식

What's new? — 뭐 새 소식이라도 있니?

솔직

No offense (is meant). — 악의로 말하는 것은 아니지만.

Give it to me straight. — 솔직하게 말해줘.

순조로움

The coast is clear. — 아무 방해자도 없다.

습관

Some people never learn. — 그 버릇 어디 가나.

시간

Time flies. — (작별의 상황에서) 시간 정말 잘 가네.

Time passes in a flash. — 시간이 쏜살같다.

(Only) Time will tell. — (오직) 시간이 말해주겠지.

식욕

I've got a big appetite. — 저 잘 먹어요.

신뢰

Read my lips. — 내 말 잘 들어.

실천

Actions speak louder than words. — 말보다 행동으로 보여주면 좋다.

Put your money where your mouth is! — 네 말을 행동으로 보여줘!

양보
It takes two to tango.   손뼉도 부딪혀야 소리가 난다.

연락
Don't be a stranger.   연락하고 지내자.
Let's keep in touch.   연락하고 지내자.

제한
The sky's the limit.   제한 없다.

종말
It's not the end of the world.   세상이 끝난 것은 아니잖아.

진심
I kid you not.   농담 아니야, 진심이야.
I mean it!   진심이야!

처지
Beggars can't be choosers.   찬밥 더운밥 가릴 처지가 아니다.

칭찬
Good for you!   잘했어!

호기심
Curiosity killed the cat.   호기심이 강하면 망신당할 수 있다.

회피
If you can't beat them, join them.   피할 수 없다면 즐겨라.

A. 우리말 의미에 알맞게 빈칸을 채워 표현을 완성하세요.

1. You're a ☐ life saver. 정말 많은 도움이 되었어요.
　　　　　☐ benefit

2. Can I have a ☐ saying with you? 잠시 이야기 나눌 수 있을까요?
　　　　　　☐ word

3. Can you ☐ receive a message? 메시지를 전해주시겠습니까?
　　　　☐ take

B. 다음 대화에 알맞은 표현이 되도록 빈칸을 채우세요.

4. A: Do you need some help with planning the company picnic?
　　B: Sure. Two he_____s are better than one.

　　A: 회사 야유회를 계획하는 데 도움이 필요하니?
　　B: 물론. 백짓장도 맞들면 낫잖아.

5. A: I'm flat broke.
　　B: Join the cl_____! I don't know how I'm going to make it until payday.

　　A: 나 완전 무일푼이야.
　　B: 피차 마찬가지야! 월급날까지 어떻게 버텨야 할지 모르겠어.

6. A: You're good at typing.
　　B: I've been typing for over thirty years. I guess pra_____ce makes perfect.

　　A: 타이핑을 정말 잘하시는군요.
　　B: 저는 30년 넘게 타이핑을 했습니다. 연습이 저를 숙련되게 한 것 같네요.

Answers

1. life
2. word
3. take
4. heads
5. club
6. practice

★ Real Test _ 해당 범위 연습문제

Choose the best word for the blank.

1. A: The musical "On 5th Street" is famous for its revolving stage.
   B: Revolving stage? Oh, yes. __________.
   (a) I played it by ear.
   (b) I'm booked up.
   (c) It's tied up.
   (d) It rings a bell.

2. A: I'm going nuts waiting to hear whether the universities have accepted me.
   B: __________ in there! You'll find out from them soon.
   (a) Stop
   (b) Hang
   (c) Hold
   (d) Relax

3. A: You can't be serious. She acts like a baby.
   B: I __________ you not. She'll do anything to get married.
   (a) kid
   (b) fool
   (c) play
   (d) ignore

4. A: Do you think the boss will extend my contract?
   B: __________ it. Better to just quit while you're ahead.
   (a) Forget
   (b) Hate
   (c) Change
   (d) Make

5. A: I'm really afraid of Professor Burton.
   B: Don't worry about him. His __________ is worse than his bite.
   (a) gnaw
   (b) bullet
   (c) bark
   (d) shot

Choose the best word for the blank.

6. A: Whose sweater is that?
   B: You __________ me there. I've never seen it before.
   (a) had
   (b) got
   (c) took
   (d) used

7. A: Jane! __________ meeting you here!
   B: Kathy, I didn't know you were coming, either!
   (a) Surprise
   (b) Good
   (c) Fancy
   (d) Imagine

8. A: Just tell your boss that you deserve a raise.
   B: I know I should. But, it's easier __________ than done.
   (a) got
   (b) had
   (c) said
   (d) told

9. A: How much do you make a year, Bob?
   B: That's for me to know. Mind your own __________!
   (a) work
   (b) duty
   (c) business
   (d) mission

10. A: The consumer is __________ up with poor quality products.
   B: The manufacturers need to raise their production standards.
   (a) tied
   (b) given
   (c) fed
   (d) kept

11. A: This cherry pie is absolutely delicious!

B: There's one small piece left. Be my __________.

(a) guest

(b) friend

(c) first

(d) customer

12. A: I hope they were wise in getting married so quickly.

B: Only time will __________.

(a) know

(b) tell

(c) say

(d) talk

13. A: This sales report looks great, but the content is nonsense.

B: I agree. Garbage in, garbage __________.

(a) off

(b) out

(c) down

(d) up

14. A: Marsha called in to say she can't work today because she has a toothache.

B: That's the last __________! Call her and tell her she's fired.

(a) minute

(b) angry

(c) straw

(d) patience

15. A: We're never going to win the photography contest!

B: Never say __________. Let's just keep trying.

(a) die

(b) down

(c) lie

(d) upset

Section Switch 

Our land, air, and water are slowly being poisoned by the waste we create. As a result, we are now facing waste problems in proportions beyond imagination. We dispose of our waste by storing, dumping, burying or burning it.

Translation

우리의 땅과 공기, 물 등이 우리가 만들어내는 쓰레기에 의해 서서히 오염되어 가고 있다. 결과적으로, 우리는 상상을 초월할 정도의 쓰레기 문제에 직면해 있다. 우리는 우리가 만들어내는 쓰레기를 쌓아놓거나, 갖다 버리거나, 땅에 파묻거나 소각해버리는 식으로 처리한다.

Vocabulary

be poisoned 오염되다
waste 쓰레기
as a result 결과적으로
face ~에 직면하다
in proportions ~할 정도로
beyond imagination 상상을 초월해
dispose of ~을 처리하다, 제거하다
store ~을 쌓아두다, 저장하다
dump ~을 버리다
bury ~을 파묻다
burn ~을 태우다

Chapter 7

내용 혼동어

TEPS에서 출제되는 내용 혼동어는 우리말 해석으로는 거의 같아 보이지만 실제 영어에서는 명확한 차이를 띠고 있는 말들이라고 정의내릴 수 있다. 이처럼 영어 어휘를 익힐 때는 각 단어가 갖는 뉘앙스의 차이를 파악할 수 있어야 한다.

A. 다음 중 우리말에 적절한 어휘를 골라 체크하세요.

1. new year's ☐ resolution 새해의 결심
☐ determination

2. train ☐ road 철길
☐ track

3. ☐ school of fish 물고기 떼
☐ pride

4. today's ☐ climate report 오늘의 일기예보
☐ weather

5. manufacturing ☐ glitch 제조상의 결함
☐ fault

B. 다음 문장에 어울리는 어휘를 고르세요.

6. You shouldn't have (interrupted / bothered) the meeting.
네가 회의를 방해해선 안 되었어.

7. Can I have a student (lent / loan)?
학자금을 대출 받을 수 있나요?

8. The Soviet Union succeeded in launching a (manned / staffed) spacecraft.
소련은 유인 우주선을 발사하는 데에 성공했다.

Answers

1. resolution
2. track
3. school
4. weather
5. glitch
6. interrupted
7. loan
8. manned

650 돌파를 위해서 꼭 구별해야 할 내용 혼동어

가깝다	close	사이가 가깝다 *cf.* close acquaintance 가까운 사이의 사람
	tight	물리적으로 가깝다
가능성	possibility	발생 가능성
	potential	잠재 가능성
	prospect	(장래의) 가망
가치	merit	장점, 취할 점
	price	가격
	value	가치, 유용성, 진가
	worth	정신적, 무형적 가치(특히 of 뒤에 오는 것에 주의)
개요/요점	abstract	어떤 글을 요약하거나 발췌하는 것
	gist	(논문, 일 따위의) 상세한 설명이 없는 요점, 요지
	outline	간략한 요강, 개요
거리	distance	물리적 의미의 단순 거리
	way	거리가 멀다고 할 때의 거리
격차	crevice	갈라진 틈
	gap	격차
	margin	득표차
결심	determination	어떤 일이나 정책 사업에 대한 결심
	resolution	마음을 잡는 것 *cf.* new year's resolution 새해의 결심
결함	cavity	충치
	dent	흠집
	glitch	(제조상의) 결함
	loophole	법망 등의 맹점
고려	attribute	~으로 돌리다, ~의 탓으로 하다
	consider	숙고하다, 두루 생각하다
	reflect	곰곰히 생각하다
	regard	주목해서 보다, 중시하다

내용 혼동어

| 고발하다 | accuse | 고발하다(전치사 of와 함께 씀) |
| | charge | 고발하다(전치사 with와 함께 씀) |

○ 오답 피하기 | accuse charge (X)

| | impeach | 고발하다; 탄핵하다(전치사 for와 함께 씀) |
| | indict | 기소하다(전치사 for와 함께 씀) |

고용하다	appoint	지명하다, 임명하다
	elect	투표로 선출하다
	hire	일시적으로 고용하다, 돈을 주고 의뢰하다
	recruit	새 회원을 들이다, 신입사원을 모집하다

| 고치다 | amend | 법조문 등을 고치다 |

ex. amend a bill 법령을 개정하다   amend constitution 헌법을 개정하다

	mend	수리하다, 수선하다
	repair	수리하다
	revamp	개조하다, 개편하다

관계/관련	chemistry	서로 손발이 잘 맞는 관계
	involvement	일에 관련 또는 연루되었는지 여부
	relation	지위 상의 상호 관계

교체/교환	barter	물물교환하다
	change	바꾸다, 갈아입다
	convert	변환하다
	exchange	교역하다, 교환하다, 맞바꾸다
	transfer	부서를 옮기다, 전직하다, 양도하다, 명의 변경하다

구분하다	classify	등급으로 나누다
	discriminate	식별하다; 구별하다
	distinguish	분별[식별]하다

| 금지하다 | ban | 금지 |
| | embargo | 선박의 출항금지 |

기간	period	기간
	quarter	4분의 1, 분기
	term	임기

기본/기초	elementary	기본의, 초보의
	preliminary	예비의, 준비의; 임시의
	primary	첫째의, 제 1의, 근본적인

길	passage	통로
	path	두 점을 연결한 길
	route	통한다는 의미에서의 길 *cf.* alternative route 다른 경로
	track	특히 철길은 train track이라고 함 *cf.* on the right track 주제에 맞는
	way	광범위한 의미의 길, 방법의 의미로 쓰임

나누다	allot	할당하다
	share	공유하다, 함께하다, 전체 중 개인의 부담
	sort	종류로 나누다, 분류하다
	quota	쿼터, 할당받은 몫

| **나머지** | debris | 잔해 |
| | residue | 제거하고 남은 부분 |

| **날씨** | climate | (장기적) 기후 |
| | weather | (단기적) 날씨 |

냄새	aroma	커피향 같은 은은한 향기
	fragrance	꽃향기 등의 일반적 향기
	odor	악취일 때

늘리다	extend	주로 기간을 연장하다
	lengthen	물리적으로 늘리다
	prolong	수명을 늘리다 *cf.* prolong life 수명을 연장하다
	spread	소문이나 전염병, 불이 퍼지다
	stretch	늘리다 *cf.* stretch imagination 상상력을 키우다

능력	ability	할 수 있는 힘, 솜씨
	aptitude	경향, 습성, 적성
	capability	능력, 역량
	versatility	다재다능

내용 혼동어

| 다른 거 | alternative | 대안 |
| | substitute | 대체물 |

다시 시작하다	relapse	다시 악화되다
	renew	갱생시키다; ~의 기한을 연장하다
	resume	다시 차지하다, 다시 시작하다

다양한	assorted	다채로운, 잡다한; 한데 섞어 담은
	diverse	가지각색의, 여러 가지의
	select	가려낸, 정선한 *cf.* selection 선발된 사람, 발췌

도달하다	plateau	정점
	reach	목표 지점에 도달하다 (예를 들어서 온도)
	score	점수가 도달하다

| 만나다 | bump into | 우연히 만나다 (반드시 into와 같이 써야 함) |
| | see | 특별한 약속을 잡고 만나다 |

만들다	create	등장인물을 만든다든지 하는 다소 창조적인 만들기
	form	의견 등을 만들다, 형성하다
	make	일반적 의미의 만들다

말하다	say	말하다, 이야기하다
	speak	언어를 구사하다
	talk	(일상적 의미의) 말하다, 말을 건네다
	tell	(아무에게) 들려주다, 고하다, 알리다 *cf.* tell the truth 진실을 말하다

면	aspect	양상, 견해
	facet	(결정체, 보석의) 작은 면, 깎은 면
	phase	(발달, 변화의) 단계, 국면

| 면제 | exempt | 면제된 |
| | free | 면제되어서 자유로운 |

| 무디다 | nebulous | 흐릿한 |
| | rusty | 무뎌진 |

무리	band	어떤 목적으로 모인 무리, 한 무리의 사람들
	crowd	군중
	flock	새, 사람의 무리
	herd	소, 돼지의 떼
	pride	사자나 공작의 떼
	school	물고기, 고래 등의 떼
받다	accept	(취급하다의 의미에서의) 받다 *cf.* accept credit cards 신용카드를 받다
	receive	(수령하다의 의미에서의) 받다
발견/인식	catch	발견해서 이해하다
	discover	먼저 발견하다
	find	(우연히) 찾아내다, 찾아서 발견하다
	spot	보고 알아내다
발생하다	happen	일반적 의미의 발생하다
	occur	자연재해 등이 발생하다(주로 to와 함께 쓰임)
변경	modify	개선을 위해 수정하다, 조정하다
	reverse	반대로 하다, 역류하다
방해하다	bother	방해하다, 귀찮게 하다(주로 사람을 목적어로 씀)
		cf. Sorry to bother you. 죄송합니다.
	interrupt	방해하다, 대화 도중에 끼어들다(사물/사람 둘 다에 씀)
		cf. You're not interrupting anything. 당신이 방해하고 있는 것은 아닙니다.
배포	circulate	회의의 의제를 다른 사람에게 돌리다
	propagate	사상 등을 보급하다
	release	개봉하거나 발표하다
	spread	병이나 소문이 퍼지다
범위	range	일반적 의미의 범위
	sight	시야
	visibility	시계 *cf.* zero visibility 시계 제로
법률	legal	법률의
	legitimate	합법적인

내용 혼동어

| **보충하다** | complement | 보충하다 |
| | supplement | 영양제 *cf.* **dietary supplement** 영양제, 식이 보조제 |

비용	charge	부담, 요금, 청구금액
	cost	소모되는 비용, 지불하는 비용
	price	물건의 가격
	rate	경우에 따라서 바뀌는 요금(특히 시즌별로)

비율	proportion	전체에 대비한 비율
	rate	특정 기간 내의 특정 횟수
	ratio	양자 비교 시의 비율

빌다, 빌리다	borrow	(돈, 물건 등을) 잠시 빌리다
	lease	(기간을 상당히 두고) 빌리다
	lend	(돈, 물건 등을) 빌려주다
	loan	(은행 등에서 돈을) 융자받다, (도서관에서 책을) 대출하다
	mortgage	주택 담보 대출을 받다
	rent	(주택을) 임차하다, (책, 비디오, 자동차 등을) 빌리다

| **사고** | accident | 교통사고 등의 인적, 재산적 피해를 수반한 사고 |
| | incident | 일반적 의미의 사고 |

사라지다	disappear	사라지다
	fade	점차 사라지다
	vanish	완전히 사라지다 *cf.* **vanish into the air** 허공으로 사라지다

사람	manned	유인의 *cf.* **manned spacecraft** 유인 우주선
	peopled	사람이 사는
	populated	사람이 거주하는
	staffed	직원이 있는

새롭게 하다	refresh	상쾌하게 하다, 기운 나게 하다
	refurbish	낡은 것을 새롭게 가공해서 만들다
	renovate	개선하다, 고쳐 만들다
	revise	교정하다, 재검사하다

생각	mind	정신(머리로 생각하는 것을 뜻함) *cf.* Great minds think alike. 나랑 생각이 똑같구나.
	thought	생각
선/길	lane	도로의 차선
	line	일반적 의미의 선
	row	좌석 줄; 여러 개로 늘어선 줄
섞다	blend	섞이는 종류가 다른 것이 섞일 때
	mix	섞이는 종류가 같을 때
설치	establish	제도를 정비하다, 제정하다
	found	(회사나 단체를) 설립하다
	furnish	가구를 비치하다
	install	기계나 소프트웨어를 설치하다
소비/낭비	consume	에너지나 시간을 소비하다, 술이나 음식물을 소비하다
	deplete	자원을 고갈시키다
	exhaust	(사람을) 녹초가 되게 하다
	waste	낭비하다
수익	benefit	이익으로서의 수익
	return	투자에 대한 대가로서의 수익
시작	opener	공연에서 개막을 알리는 사람
	starter	음식에 처음 나오는 것
신청	enroll	등록시키다
	sign up for	등록하다
	take	등록하다(전치사 없이 그냥 씀)
실수	error	무의식 중의 실수
	fault	과실적 의미가 강하다
	mistake	시험 등에서의 실수, 실패

내용 혼동어

실시/시행	enforce	(법률 등을) 실시[시행]하다, 집행하다
	excute	직무를 완수하다, 사형을 집행하다
	implement	(약속 따위를) 이행하다
	operate	작동시키다, 수술하다
실패	backfire	(계획이) 실패하다
	breakdown	고장; 파괴
	collapse	무너지다
	debacle	총체적 실패
없음	invalid	실효성이 없는, (법적으로) 무효
	void	빈, 공허한
	zero	최하점; 밑바닥; 무(無)
연속적인	consecutive	일이 연속적으로 일어나는 것
	consecutive holiday	연휴
	continuous	끊임없는
	periodic	주기적인
영역	boundary	지역, 공원의 영역
	territory	영토
접시	dish	음식 담는 접시
	plate	큰 접시
	saucer	찻잔 받침 접시
	tray	쟁반 같은 접시
중요 물건/사건	breakthrough	오랫동안의 시도 끝에 갑자기 발생한 획기적 발전
	landmark	획기적인 사건, 유명한 건물이나 장소
	milestone	이정표, 처음 행해진 중요한 사건
	turning point	전환점
측정하다	appraise	(재산의 금전적 가치를) 전문적으로 평가하다
	estimate	추정치로서 가치 · 수량 등을 어림잡다
	measure	측량하다

치료	cure	병을 치료하다
	treat	상처를 치료하다
친구	colleague	직업상 동료
	companion	동반자 개념의 친구
	company	동료, 동반자 개념의 친구

ex. Misery loves company. 동병상련이다.

I'm expecting company. 손님을 기다리고 있다.

투표	ballot	투표 용지
	poll	여론 조사
	vote	투표
할당하다	allowance	용돈; 허용량; 보수
	dividend	이익 배당금
	installment	할부금의 1회분
	quata	배급
환불	rebate	이미 지급한 금액의 일부를 환불하다, (일부) 환불
	refund	물건 값을 되돌려 주다, 환불
	reimburse	앞서 쓴 금액을 나중에 보상 · 변상하다

A. 우리말에 맞는 적절한 어휘를 골라 체크하세요.

1. ☐ prolong life expectancy 평균 수명을 연장하다
☐ extend

2. ☐ furnish a program 프로그램을 설치하다
☐ install

3. ☐ prolong imagination 상상력을 펼치다
☐ stretch

B. 다음 문장에 어울리는 어휘를 고르세요.

4. Suddenly an earthquake (occurred / raised).
갑자기 지진이 발생했다.

5. The prosecutor (impeached / accused) him for robbery.
검사는 그 남자를 강도죄로 기소했다.

6. The strict father (enrolled / assigned) his son into military school.
그 엄격한 아버지는 아들을 군사학교에 등록시켰다.

Answers
1. prolong
2. install
3. stretch
4. occurred
5. accused
6. enrolled

★ Real Test _ 해당 범위 연습문제

Choose the best word for the blank.

1. A: Have we __________ our fund raising target yet?
   B: In fact, a donation from an anonymous person has helped us to meet that goal.
   (a) reached
   (b) scored
   (c) arrived
   (d) rewarded

2. The Japanese government has been concerned about the low birth __________ since the late 1990's.
   (a) rate
   (b) ratio
   (c) percentage
   (d) proportion

3. A military jury found a soldier guilty of rape and murder in the slaying of a 14-year-old Iraqi girl and her family, despite testimony that cast doubt on his __________.
   (a) engagement
   (b) involvement
   (c) relation
   (d) chemistry

4. The environmental group held a public meeting, hoping to draw support for a __________ on constructing a new factory along the river.
   (a) ban
   (b) embargo
   (c) provocation
   (d) taboo

5. The pilot had reported zero __________ outside, which was caused by the storm.
   (a) visibility
   (b) sight
   (c) range
   (d) limit

★Random Test _ 모든 범위의 연습문제

Choose the best word for the blank.

6. A: With her new hair style, I didn't __________ that she was the boss's wife.
B: Join the club. If she heard that, she would take it as a compliment.
(a) realize
(b) notice
(c) recognize
(d) know

7. A: I would like to see Ms. Barker.
B: Do you have an __________?
(a) appointment
(b) arrangement
(c) commitment
(d) promise

8. A: I would like to see Doctor Packson.
B: Let me see when he is __________. How about 3 p.m. tomorrow?
(a) possible
(b) available
(c) accessible
(d) liable

9. A: I think we'll do better work in the afternoon if we have a nice steak for lunch.
B: You know, great minds __________ alike.
(a) think
(b) ponder
(c) recall
(d) reflect

10. A: Why is Albert so critical of everyone today?
B: He's been feeling down recently. And, you know how misery loves __________.
(a) friend
(b) company
(c) failure
(d) loser

11. A: The sales department has decided to __________ in on prospective customers under 30.

B: Does that include both men and women?

(a) target

(b) shoot

(c) zero

(d) hit

12. Even to the scientists, __________ the difference between rocks and minerals is an odd and difficult job.

(a) discriminating

(b) telling

(c) hammering out

(d) ironing out

13. Moved by the __________ of the flood victims broadcasted on TV, people from around the country donated food, blankets and clothing.

(a) plague

(b) doom

(c) dearth

(d) predicament

14. A robotic dirt and ice digger rocketed toward Mars on Saturday, beginning a 422 million-mile journey that NASA hopes will __________ next spring in the first ever landing within the red planet's Arctic Circle.

(a) culminate

(b) peak

(c) arrive

(d) come

15. My roommate accepted my proposal that we should divide the utility bills; but he has not paid his __________ yet.

(a) share

(b) lot

(c) sort

(d) quota

Section Switch

Giant pumpkins, tomatoes, and strawberries are being developed now, as well as new flowers. The techniques have created plants that resist disease, require less specific care, and grow larger seeds and fruits on fewer nutrients and water. So what began as an effort to make stronger plants may end up as a way to increase the yields of farm and garden crops.

Translation

거대한 호박과 토마토, 딸기가 신종 화훼류와 함께 현재 개발 중이다. 과학 기술은 질병에 강하고 돌보기 쉬우면서 더 적은 영양분과 물로도 더 큰 씨와 열매를 맺는 식물을 만들어냈다. 더 강한 식물을 만들어내기 위해 시작한 이 노력은 결국에는 농장과 밭의 농작물 생산량을 증가시키는 방법이 될지도 모른다.

Vocabulary

resist ~에 저항하다
disease 질병
require ~을 요구하다
specific 특별한, 세세한
care 돌봄, 보살핌
seed 씨앗
nutrient 영양분
end up 결국 ~하게 되다
yield 생산량

Chapter 8

형태 혼동어

형태 혼동어는 철자가 유사해서 의미가 혼동되는 경우를 말한다. TEPS에서는 일반 영어 시험과는 달리 미세한 차이를 보이는 철자의 단어를 요소요소에 배치해서 학생들을 곤란에 빠뜨린다.

A. 우리말에 맞는 적절한 어휘를 골라 체크하세요.

1. ☐ considerable amount 상당한 양
☐ considerate

2. breast ☐ augmentation 가슴 확대 수술
☐ argument

3. sugar ☐ canon 사탕수수
☐ cane

B. 우리말 의미에 알맞게 빈칸을 채워 표현을 완성하세요.

4. am____sia   기억상실
an____ia   빈혈증
am____tia   정신박약

5. dev____e   헌신하다, 전념하다
dev____r   게걸스럽게 먹다
dev____t   독실한, 경건한

6. dec____e   십년
dec______ence 쇠미, 타락; 퇴폐기
dec______ent   퇴폐적인, 퇴폐기의

650 돌파를 위해서 꼭 구별해야 할 형태 혼동어

abolition	폐지
abortion	임신중절
acclamation	갈채
acclimation	적응
activate	활기차게 하다
actuate	~하게 하다
adapt	적응시키다
adept	숙달한
adopt	① 채택하다, 받아들이다 ② 양자로 삼다
addition	부가(물)
addiction	중독
advance	전진, 진출, 진보
advent	다가옴, 출현, 도래
adventure	모험
adventitious	우연의, 외래의
adventurous	모험적인
adversary	적
adversity	역경, 고초
aid	도움
aide	보조자
allegiance	충성
allegation	(증거 없는) 주장
altar	(교회의) 제단, 제대
alter	변경하다

형태 혼동어

alteration	변경
alternation	교대
altercation	언쟁
alternately	교대로
alternatively	양자택일로
amaze	~을 놀라게 하다
amuse	즐겁게 하다
amenable	복종하는, 순종하는
amendable	고칠 수 있는
amnesia	기억상실
amentia	정신박약
anemia	빈혈증
anecdote	일화
antidote	해독제
anonymous	익명의
anomalous	특이한
annual	1년을 단위로 하는
annul	취소하다
annals	연보
apathy	냉담, 무심
antipathy	반감
appall	오싹하게 하다
appeal	호소하다
appraise	평가하다, 견적하다
apprise	알리다

argument	논쟁, 논거
augment	증대시키다, 증가시키다 *cf.* 명사형은 augmentation
assent	동의하다
assert	단언하다, 주장하다
assess	평가하다, 액수를 정하다
asset	자산
assort	분류하다
astronomy	천문학
astrology	점성술
attendance	출석(자)
attention	주의; 친절
autocratic	독재적인
automatic	자동의
automation	자동 조작
automaton	기계 같은 사람
axe	도끼
axis	축, 축선, 굴대
balmy	① 향긋한 ② 온화한
barmy	약간 미친
bandage	붕대
bondage	노예 상태
bare	벌거벗은
barely	가까스로
bear	곰
bass	저음부
base	기초

형태 혼동어

beatify	죽은 사람을 시복하다
beautify	아름답게 하다
beneficent	자선심이 많은
beneficial	유익한
bequeath	유증하다, 유산을 남기다
bequest	유증, 유산
beside	~의 옆에
besides	~외에도
bilateral	양쪽의
biliteral	두 자의
bland	온화한
blend	섞다
blind	눈먼, 장님의
brand	상표, 오명, 횃불
bless	은총을 빌다
bliss	기쁨, 즐거움
blink	깜박거리다, 깜작이다
brink	가장자리, 가
bloodline	혈통
bloodshed	유혈사태, 살육
bloodstain	핏자국
bloom	꽃이 피다
broom	비, 빗자루
boarder	기숙생
border	국경

boast	자랑하다
boost	① 뒤에서 밀다, 밀어 올리다, 후원, 응원
	② improve의 의미
bonny	예쁜
bony	여윈
borrow	빌리다
burrow	(짐승이 파놓은) 굴
cane	지팡이, 등나무
cannon	대포
canon	규범, 표준
canvas	강한 천
canvass	선거 운동하다, 조사하다
casualty	사상자
causality	인과관계
ceiling	천장
cell	세포
cellar	지하실
censor	검열하다, 검열관
censure	비난하다, 나무라다
census	인구조사
choir	성가대, 합창대
chore	귀찮은 허드렛일
chord	(악기의) 현, 줄
code	법규, 법전, 암호법, 약호
cord	새끼줄, 끈
chronic	상습적인; 만성인
choleric	화를 잘 내는

claim	v. 청구하다, 요구하다 n. 요구, 청구
clam	조개
cram	벼락치기 공부를 하다; 처박아 넣다
cramp	① 경련, 쥐 ② 꺾쇠
clarify	명료하게 하다, 맑게 하다
classify	분류하다, 유별하다
clash	충돌
collision	충돌
collusion	공모
commodious	공간이 넓은, 널찍한
commodity	상품, 일용품
commotion	동요, 소동
common	공동의; 일반적인
commune	교감하다
complain	불평하다
complaint	불평, 불만
comparable	비교할 만한
comparative	비교의
comprehend	이해하다
comprehensible	이해하기 쉬운
comprehensive	포괄적인; 이해력 있는
concede	인정하다, 승인하다
conceit	자만, 자기 과대평가
condemn	① 비난하다, 낙인찍다 ② 죄를 선고하다 ③ 압수하다
contemn	경멸하다

condole	애도하다
condone	용서하다, 너그럽게 보아주다
console	위로하다
consolidate	통합하다
conducive	도움이 되는
conductive	(열 등을) 전도 할 수 있는
confidant	막역한 친구
confident	확신하는
confirm	확인하다
conform	따르(게 하)다, 순응(하게)하다
congenial	마음이 맞는
congenital	선천성의
considerable	상당한, 생각할 만한, 무시 못 할
considerate	사려 깊은, 신중한
constituent	구성 요소; 선거구민
constitution	구조; 헌법; 체질
consul	영사
council	회의
counsel	조언하다
consult	조언을 구하다
contact	접촉
contract	①계약 기간, 계약서 ②축약하다, 수축하다
contagious	(병 등이) 전염의
contiguous	인접한
containment	봉쇄
contaminant	오염 물질(contaminate에서 나온 단어)

형태 혼동어

contemptible	경멸할 만한
contemptuous	경멸적인
contend	다투다, 경쟁하다
content	내용, 알갱이
contentment	만족
contention	다툼
convey	나르다, 전달하다
convoy	호위하다, 호송하다
cooperate	협력하다
corporate	법인의, 공동의
corps	군단
corpse	시체
credible	믿을 만한
credulous	쉽게 믿는
creditable	칭찬할 만한
correspondent	통신원
corespondent	(이혼 소송의) 공동 피고인
council	회의, 평의회
counsel	v. 상담하다 n. 상담
crash	충돌
crush	압착
crude	조잡한
cruel	잔인한
daily	매일의
dairy	낙농장, 낙농실, 우유점
diary	일기(장), 일지

debilitate   쇠약하게 하다
deliberate   신중한

decade   십년
decadence   쇠미, 타락; 퇴폐기
decadent   퇴폐적인, 퇴폐기의

decent   품위 있는, 점잖은, 꽤 좋은
descent   강하, 전락

decimal   십진법의
decimate   대량으로 살상하다

decoration   장식법, 꾸임새, 장식물, 훈장
decorum   예의바름, 단정함

decry   공공연히 비난하다
descry   어렴풋이[멀리] 알아보다, 발견하다

deduce   연역하다, 추론하다 *cf.* 명사형은 deduction
deduct   공제하다 *cf.* 명사형은 deduction

defer   연기하다, 양보하다
deter   저지하다, 막다

deference   복종; 존경
difference   차이

definite   명확한
deficient   부족한
definitive   최종적인, 결정적인

den   굴, 소굴
dent   움푹 패인 곳

depose	물러나게 하다, 면직시키다
deposit	축적하다
dispose	① 배열하다, 처리하다 ② 버리다 ③ 마음이 내키게 하다
deprecate	반대하다
depreciate	경시하다, 가치를 낮추다
deprive	빼앗다
deride	조롱하다
derive	끌어내다
despairing	절망적인
despondent	낙담한
device	장치, 장비
devise	고안하다
devote	헌신하다, 전념하다
devour	게걸스럽게 먹다
devout	독실한, 경건한
die	죽다
dye	염색하다
differ	다르다, 틀리다
difference	다름, 차이
different	다른
diffident	자신이 없는
diffuse	(열, 냄새 등을) 발산하다
defuse	해소하다
dim	어둠침침한, 어둑한
dime	10센트 동전
disapprove	비난하다
disprove	반증하다

disassemble	분해하다
dissemble	감추다
discreet	분별 있는, 사려 깊은, 신중한
discrete	따로따로의, 구별된
discretion	신중, 사려; 자유재량, 판단의 자유
disjoin	분리하다
disjoint	관절을 빼게 하다; 어지럽히다
disperse	흩어지게 하다
dispense	분배하다; 조제하다
distinct	다른
distinctive	독특한
dismal	우울한, 쓸쓸한
dismiss	해고하다, 떠나게 하다
diverse	다른
divert	(목적 등을) 바꾸다
docile	온순한, 유순한
domicile	처소, 집, 주거
dual	이중의
duel	결투
dull	무딘
dully	둔하게, 느리게
duly	정식으로, 정당하게
dumb	멍청한, 벙어리의
dump	(쓰레기를) 내버리다
dyeing	염색
dying	죽어가는

형태 혼동어

economic	경제의
economical	절약하는
elemental	기본적인
elementary	초보의
enlighten	계몽시키다, 각성시키다
enliven	활기를 띠게 하다
enormity	극악
enormous	거대한
entitle	~에게 자격을 주다
entity	존재물
epidemic	유행
epidermic	표피의
erratic	이상한
erotic	호색의
ethnic	민족의
ethical	윤리[도덕]의
evade	피하다, 거부하다
evolve	발전하다, 진화하다
exactly	정확히
exacting	(요구 등이) 엄한
exalt	높이다
exult	크게 기뻐하다
expel	몰아내다, 축출하다
extol	칭찬하다
extort	강탈하다, 억지로 자백을 받아내다

explicit	명백한, 뚜렷이 말한
exploit	업적
facility	편리, 설비, 솜씨
felicity	큰 행복
ferocity	잔인성
faint	① 희미한, 힘없는, 어지러운 ② 실신하다
feint	치는 시늉을 하다, 견제 공격을 하다
fair	n. 박람회, 시장 a. 공평한, 맑은
fare	운임
fertile	비옥한
futile	쓸데없는, 무익한
flap	치다
flip	손끝으로 가볍게 치다
flight	비행
freight	운송화물
fright	공포
plight	곤경, 역경
forbear	참다
forebear	조상
forceful	힘 있는
forcible	강제적인, 억지로 시키는
formally	정식으로
formerly	이전에는
fragile	깨지기 쉬운
frail	연약한, 무른

function	기능
fluctuation	(방향, 위치, 상황 등의) 변동, 오르내림
funeral	장례식
funnel	바늘구멍, 깔때기
genteel	상류 사회의
gentle	온화한
gentile	(유대인 입장에서의) 이교도의
genuine	진짜의
genius	천재
geography	지리학
geology	지질학
german	같은 부모에게서 태어난
germane	적절한
gest	(중세의 운문의) 모험담
gist	요지
ghastly	무서운, 소름끼치는
ghostly	유령의
gloss	광택
glossy	광택이 있는
gross	총계의; 뚱뚱한
glow	백열, 작열
grow	자라다
granite	화강암
graphite	그래파이트, 석묵, 흑연

grateful	감사하는
gratuitous	무료의
gratifying	만족을 주는
grisly	섬뜩한
grizzly	회색의
hallow	~을 신성하게 하다
hollow	속이 비게 하다
healthy	건강한
healthful	건강에 좋은
historic	역사상 중요한
historical	역사의
histrionic	꾸민 듯한
hoist	v. 들어 올리다 n. 화물 승강기
host	주인; 무리, 떼
hostel	숙박소
hostile	적의 있는
human	사람의
humane	자비로운
humid	습기 있는, 누기 찬
humiliate	자존심을 상하게 하다
humility	겸손
imaginary	상상 속의
imaginative	상상력이 풍부한
immunity	면역(성)
impunity	형벌을 받지 않음

형태 혼동어

impair	해치다
impart	주다
impartial	공정한, 치우침이 없는
importable	수입될 수 있는
impotable	마실 수 없는
important	중요한
impotent	무력한
inapt	부적절한
inept	서투른
incident	일어난 일, 사건
incidence	발생 정도[범위], 율
incidental	부수하여 일어나는, 흔히 발생하는
indigenous	고유의
indigent	가난한
indignant	분개하는
induce	유도하다; 귀납하다
induct	안내하다, 앉히다
industrial	산업의
industrious	근면한
insolent	건방진, 오만한
insolvent	지불 불능의, 파산한
intelligent	총명한
intelligible	쉽게 이해되는
intension	강화, 긴장
intention	의도

intimate	친밀, 친분이 두터운
intimidate	위협하다
intricate	복잡한
intrigue	~의 호기심을 돋우다, 음모
intrude	침입하다, 밀고 들어가다
judicial	재판의
judicious	신중한
keen	날카로운, 예리한
kin	친족, 친척
liberal	관대한
literal	문자 그대로의
literate	읽고 쓸 줄 아는
literary	문학의
loose	풀어진
lose	잃어버리다
mass	집단
mess	혼란
massage	안마
message	전갈
mediate	(분쟁 등을) 조정하다
meditate	숙고하다
moral	도덕의
morale	사기
momentary	순간의
momentous	중대한

형태 혼동어

negligent	태만한
negligible	사소한
notify	알리다
notice	알아차리다
official	공적인
officious	(쓸데없이) 참견하는
past	과거
paste	밀가루 반죽
personal	개인의
personnel	직원
portable	휴대용의, 들고 다닐 수 있는
potable	마시기에 적합한
prescribe	명령하다, 지시하다, 규정하다
proscribe	금지하다, 배척하다
primary	으뜸가는, 제일의
primate	영장류
raise	(들어)올리다
rise	오르다; 증가하다
respectable	존경할 만한
respectful	경의를 표하는
respective	각각의, 각기의
rub	① 문지르다, 긁다 ② 탁본하다
rubbish	쓰레기, 폐물
sailer	배
sailor	선원

saw	① see의 과거 ② 톱
sew	깁다, 꿰매다
sow	씨를 뿌리다
shallow	얕은, 천박한
swallow	① 제비 ② 삼키다
statue	상, 조상
stature	키, 신장
statute	법령
status	지위, 신분, 법률상의 신분
temperate	온난한, 온화한
temporary	일시의, 임시의
tendency	경향
tender	부드러운
touch	감동을 주다
tough	어려운
variable	변하기 쉬운
various	다양한
virtual	실질적인
virtue	선행, 선
virtuous	고결한
waive	(권리 등을) 포기하다
wave	물결
wholesale	대규모의, 도매
wholesome	건전한, 유익한

A. 다음 문장에 어울리는 어휘를 고르세요.

1. As he is used to being hurt by a lot of words, the boy won't be (intimidated / intimate) by such a bluff.

많은 말에 상처를 받는 데 익숙해져 있기 때문에 그 소년은 그런 엄포는 겁내지 않을 것이다.

2. His (function / fluctuations) when confronted with a problem annoyed all of us who had to wait until he made his decision.

문제에 직면했을 때 그의 우유부단함은 그가 결정을 내릴 때까지 기다려야 하는 우리 모두를 화나게 했다.

3. Reverence for one's (forebears / forbears) plays an important part in many Oriental cultures.

조상들에 대한 존경은 많은 동양 문화에서 중요한 역할을 한다.

4. This plant is grown in (futile / fertile) land.

이 식물은 비옥한 땅에서 자란다.

5. He has a (keen / kin) interest in politics.

그는 정치에 대하여 예리한 관심을 가지고 있다.

B. 다음 중 우리말에 적절한 어휘를 골라 체크하세요.

6. night ☐ cessation 심야회의
       ☐ session

7. ☐ judicial court 법정
  ☐ judicious

8. save the ☐ sailer 선원을 구조하다
        ☐ sailor

Answers

1. intimidated
2. fluctuations
3. forebears
4. fertile
5. keen
6. session
7. judicial
8. sailor

★ **Real Test** _ 해당 범위 연습문제

Choose the best word for the blank.

1. A: What did eventually earn Edison $40,000, a ___________ sum at the time?
   B: He made an improvement on the existing stock ticker.
   (a) considerable
   (b) considering
   (c) considerable
   (d) considerated

2. John will ___________ the papers, hunting for notices of jobs.
   (a) canvass
   (b) canvas
   (c) converse
   (d) compass

3. The legendary accomplishments of Paul Bunyan and Pecos Bill are ___________,
   while the so-called legends about Washington and Lincoln are mostly exaggerations
   of real qualities which those two presidents had.
   (a) imaginable
   (b) imaginary
   (c) imagined
   (d) imaginative

4. The Japanese often tried cross-___________ travel when the exchange rate was
   preferable to them.
   (a) border
   (b) country
   (c) examining
   (d) over

5. Government officials suspected an illegal ___________ in the big merger deal.
   (a) collusion
   (b) collision
   (c) corrosion
   (d) corroboration

★Random Test _ 모든 범위의 연습문제

Choose the best word for the blank.

6. A: I was driving back home when I saw a red car following but then it suddenly disappeared.
B: I don't think anybody was following you. You are just getting __________.
(a) parallel
(b) paranormal
(c) paralyzed
(d) paranoid

7. A: Today's math exam was a breeze.
B: Oh, stop being so __________.
(a) overconfident
(b) overburdened
(c) overrated
(d) overdone

8. The post office will be closed next Monday in __________ of Memorial Day.
(a) observation
(b) reservation
(c) regulation
(d) observance

9. Tim hoped that the value of his stamp collection would __________, but it has become worthless.
(a) perish
(b) subside
(c) appreciate
(d) depreciate

10. During his speech, the President __________ the need for a global approach to environmental problems several times.
(a) underscored
(b) underwent
(c) undermined
(d) undertook

11. Science itself is morally neutral, that is, __________ to the value of the ends for which the means are used.
    (a) different
    (b) indifferent
    (c) interested
    (d) uninteresting

12. My parents were determined to teach my little sister to behave __________ in church, although it made them nervous to sit through a long service while she squirmed between them on the pew.
    (a) respectively
    (b) respectably
    (c) respectfully
    (d) respectingly

13. Betty's mother sent her to the best __________ in town for her sports injuries.
    (a) orthopedist
    (b) orthodontist
    (c) optician
    (d) oculist

14. The __________ of people from big cities to the country reaches a peak in the first week of August.
    (a) exertion
    (b) exodus
    (c) extinction
    (d) excess

15. Against her doctor's orders, the woman continued to work overtime, to the __________ of her health.
    (a) depreciation
    (b) demolition
    (c) detriment
    (d) derision

Section Switch

In 1927 Werner Heisenberg announced that, in subatomic experiments, the very act of observation distorts reality in such a way that one can determine either the position or the velocity of a particle, but never both at once. Reality is loosed from its moorings, and the human observer becomes an agent in determining what's there.

Translation

1927년 베르너 하이젠버그는 소립자 실험에서, 입자의 위치나 속도 중 하나를 확정할 수는 있어도 두 가지를 동시에 모두 확정할 수는 없기에 관찰 행위 자체가 실재를 왜곡해버린다고 발표했다. (관찰 행위로 인해) 실재는 그 실재가 존재하는 곳에서 흐트러지게 되고, 관찰자는 사실을 결정하는 데 개입되는 요소가 되어버리는 것이다.

Vocabulary

subatomic 소립자의 *cf.* subatomic particle 소립자
determine ~을 결정하다, 확정하다
observation 관찰 *cf.* observer 관찰자
distort ~을 왜곡하다
velocity 속도
particle 입자
be loosed 흐트러지다, 느슨해지다
mooring 배가 정박해 있는 곳. 여기서는 비유적으로 쓰임.
agent 개입자, 관여자

Chapter 9

다의어

다의어란 말 그대로 하나의 단어가 여러 가지의 다른 의미를 가지고 있는 경우를 말한다. 물론 여러 가지 의미를 가진다는 것은 영어의 특징이고 TEPS에서는 그 점에 주목해 어휘 영역의 문제를 집중적으로 출제하지만, 특히 이 책에서 다의어로 별도로 설정한 본 Chapter에서는 하나의 단어가 3가지 이상의 의미로 자주 활용되는 경우를 주로 다루도록 한다.

A. 다음 단어에 대해 괄호 안에 적힌 기본적인 의미 외에 잘 쓰이는 의미를 최소한 두 개 써보세요.

1. age (나이) _________________

____

2. face (얼굴) _________________

____

3. capital (수도, 자본) _________________

____

4. air (공기) _________________

____

B. 다음에 공통으로 들어갈 단어를 쓰세요.

5. The lion took a b__e at the explorer.
How about a b__e to eat after we finish the project?

6. Who is cond_____ting the orchestra this evening?
Mr. Johnson cond_____ted the visitors around the museum.

7. We shall have to s__e up if we want to go to Florida this summer.
A word processor will s__e you all this trouble.

5. 사자가 그 탐험가를 물려고 달려들었다.
프로젝트를 끝낸 다음에 뭐 좀 먹으러 갈까?

6. 오늘 저녁에는 누가 관현악단을 지휘할 것인가?
Johnson씨는 방문객들을 박물관으로 안내했다.

7. 우리는 이번 여름에 플로리다로 가기를 원한다면 저축해야만 할 것이다.
워드 프로세서는 이 모든 번거로움을 없애줄 것이다.

Answers

1. 시대, 성년
2. 액면, 직면하다
3. 뛰어난, 사형의
4. 뽐내는 꼴, 방송하다
5. bite
6. conduct
7. save

650 돌파를 위해서 꼭 외워야 할 다의어

account

기본의미	① n. 거래, 구좌, 계좌
	② v. 밝히다, 설명하다(explain)
	③ n. 묘사, 설명(description)
TEPS 중요의미	④ n. 중요성
	⑤ n. 중요한 사람
	⑥ n. 참작, 고려(consideration)
	⑦ n. 이유
	⑧ n. 일
	⑨ n. 조건
	⑩ v. 차지하다

act

기본의미	① n. 행동, 행위(doing something, action)
	② v. 행동하다
	③ n. (연극의) 막
TEPS 중요의미	④ v. 연기하다, 꾸며내다(make up)
	⑤ v. 작용하다, 효과를 내다(affect)
	⑥ v. 대체하다

address

기본의미	① n. 주소(the number or name of the house or building)
	② v. 연설하다, 성명을 발표하다(speech)
	③ n. 연설, 강연(speech)
	④ v. 말을 걸다(talk to), 부르다, 호칭하다
TEPS 중요의미	⑤ v. 부합하다(to match, correspond)
	⑥ v. 토의하다, 다루다(discuss)
	⑦ v. 전념하다

affect

기본의미	① v. 영향을 미치다
TEPS 중요의미	② v. 상처를 내다

다의어

age
기본의미　① n. 시대(era)

TEPS 중요의미　② n. 성년(the age when you are legally old enough to do something)
③ n. 오랜 시간 *ex.* It's been ages. 오랜만이야.

agent
기본의미　① n. 대리인(representative), 중개인, 지배인

TEPS 중요의미　② n. 발동자, 행위자, 동작자
③ n. 힘(force), 작용물, 작용 약제(a chemical or substance that is used for a particular purpose)

aim
기본의미　① v. 겨냥하다, 겨누다(set one's sight)
② v. ~을 목표로 하다, ~을 목표로 삼다(set a goal)
③ n. 겨냥(pointing)
④ n. 목표, 목적(purpose)

TEPS 중요의미　⑤ v. ~하려고 하다, ~할 작정이다(intend, mean)

air
기본의미　① n. 공기, 대기
② n. 하늘, 공중(sky)
③ n. 분위기(atmosphere)

TEPS 중요의미　④ n. 외견(appearance), 모양, 풍채, 태도
⑤ v. 방송하다(broadcast)
⑥ v. 뽐내다(cause others to know)

apply
기본의미　① v. 신청하다, 지원하다

TEPS 중요의미　② v. 전념하게 하다, 몰두하게 하다, 집중시키다(concentrate)

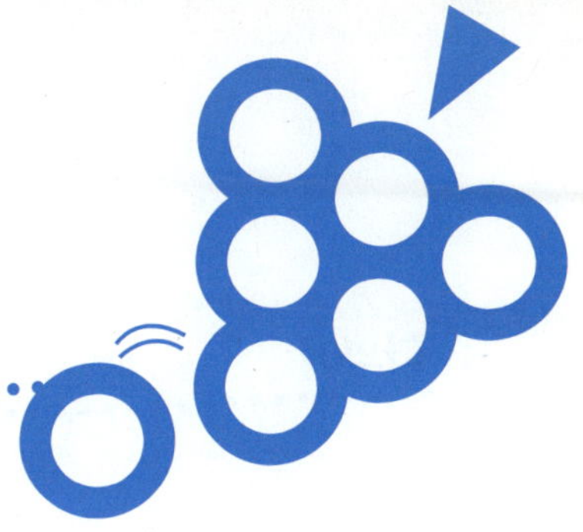

approach

기본의미	① v. (장소, 사람 등에) 접근하다(come near to)
	② v. (성질, 상태, 시간, 정도 등이) ~에 가까워지다, ~에 가깝다
	③ n. 다가옴, 근사, 유사, 접근
TEPS 중요의미	④ v. 시작하다, 착수하다(begin)

arrange

기본의미	① v. 정리하다, 정돈하다(place in proper order)
	② v. (행사 등과 관련해 일정이나 제반사항들을) 미리 준비하다, 정하다
	③ v. ~을 해결하다, 조정하다(adjust or settle)
TEPS 중요의미	④ v. 편곡하다, 각색하다(adapt)

art

기본의미	① n. 예술
	② n. 요령, 기술(technique)
TEPS 중요의미	③ n. 계략, 책략(trick)
	④ n. 방법

associate

기본의미	① v. ~와 어울리다, 교제하다(consort)
	② v. ~을 동료로 참가시키다, 연합시키다(join, unite)
	③ v. 제휴자, 공동 경영자, 동료(partner, colleague)
TEPS 중요의미	④ v. 연상하다, 연결 지어 생각하다(to connect in the mind)

assume

기본의미	① v. 생각하다
	② v. 맡다
TEPS 중요의미	③ v. 척하다
	④ v. 표정을 띠다
	⑤ v. 가정하다

다의어

attack

기본의미	① v. 공격하다, 습격하다(assault)
	② v. 비난하다, 힐뜯다(criticize)
TEPS 중요의미	③ v. 달려들다, 착수하다(set to)
	④ n. 개시, 시작(launch)

attend

기본의미	① v. ~에 참석하다, 동반하다(take part in, accompany)
	② v. ~에 주의를 기울이다(pay attention)
TEPS 중요의미	③ v. ~을 돌보다, 처리하다(take care of)
	④ v. ~에 수반하다, 따르다(come after)

bear

기본의미	① n. 곰
	② v. 낳다(give birth to)
	③ v. 참다, 견디다(endure, tolerate, put up with)
TEPS 중요의미	④ v. 지탱하다(support)
	⑤ v. 나르다(carry)
	⑥ v. 갖다(hold)
	⑦ v. (열매를) 맺다, 꽃이 피다(bring forth, bloom)
	⑧ n. 관련성(bearings)

benefit

기본의미	① n. 이익(good, interest, advantage)
TEPS 중요의미	② n. 보험금(insurance money)

betray

기본의미	① v. ~을 배반하다, 배신하다(be unfaithful to)
TEPS 중요의미	② v. (비밀을) 누설하다, 폭로하다(give away, expose)
	③ v. (감정, 의도를) 나타내다, 드러내다(reveal), 태도를 띠다

bite

기본의미	① v. 물다, 깨물어 자르다, 물어뜯다(seize or tear with the teeth)
	② v. 미끼를 물다, 미끼에 걸리다
	③ n. 물기, 물어뜯기
TEPS 중요의미	④ n. 음식, 먹을 것(food)

buy

기본의미	① v. 사다(purchase, get)
TEPS 중요의미	② n. 구매(잘 샀다는 의미)
	③ v. 믿다(believe, put belief in)
	④ v. 벌다(earn, make)

capital

기본의미	① n. 수도
	② n. 대문자
	③ n. 자금, 자본, 자본금(money, funds)
TEPS 중요의미	④ a. 뛰어난(excellent)
	⑤ a. 사형의, 죽음에 해당하는, 치명적인(deadly)

cast

기본의미	① v. 던지다
	② v. (연극에서) 역할을 주다, 역을 맡기다(assign a role)
	③ v. ~을 만들다, 주조하다(found, mint)
TEPS 중요의미	④ v. 합하다
	⑤ n. 깁스

catch

기본의미	① v. 잡다
	② v. 의미를 이해하다
TEPS 중요의미	③ v. 병에 걸리다
	④ n. 조건
	⑤ n. 속셈

다의어

cause

기본의미	① n. 이유
TEPS 중요의미	② n. 대의명분

change

기본의미	① n. 잔돈(small change, loose money)
	② n. 거스름 돈
	③ n. 변경, 수정, 변화(alteration)
	④ v. 변하다(vary)
	⑤ v. 옷을 갈아입다(change one's clothes)
TEPS 중요의미	⑥ v. 자리를 바꾸다

check

기본의미	① v. 조사하다, 검사하다, 확인하다(examine)
	② n. 수표
TEPS 중요의미	③ v. 저지하다, 방해하다(obstruct)

circulation

기본의미	① n. 혈액 순환
	② n. (화폐 등의) 유통, (소식 등의) 유포
TEPS 중요의미	③ n. (신문, 잡지 등의) 발행 부수, 판매 부수
	④ n. 대출

command

기본의미	① v. 지휘하다, 명령하다(direct)
	② n. 명령, 지시(order)
TEPS 중요의미	③ n. (언어의) 구사력
	④ n. 전망(view, outlook)
	⑤ v. (존경, 동정 등을) 받다

conduct

기본의미	① n. 행동, 행위(behavior)
	② v. 행동하다, 처신하다(act, behave)
TEPS 중요의미	③ v. 지휘하다(command)
	④ v. 수행하다
	⑤ v. 안내하다(usher, guide, lead)

content

기본의미	① a. 만족한, 흡족한(satisfied)
	② v. 만족시키다(satisfy)
TEPS 중요의미	③ n. 내용(the subject matter of a book, speech)
	④ n. 차례, 목차, 항목

contract

기본의미	① n. 계약(agreement)
	② n. 계약서, 약정서(contract document)
	③ v. 계약을 맺다(make a contract)
	④ v. 수축되다, 축소하다(lessen)
	⑤ v. 좁아지다(narrow)
TEPS 중요의미	⑥ v. 병에 걸리다(catch)
	⑦ v. 빚지다(owe)

count

기본의미	① v. 세다(calculate)
	② v. 생각하다, 간주하다(think, consider, regard)
	③ v. 중요하다(matter, be important)
	④ v. 꼽히다
TEPS 중요의미	⑤ v. 포함시키다(include)
	⑥ v. (~의) 수[양]에 달하다, (~가) 되다(reach, come to)
	⑦ v. 의지하다(count on)

다의어

cover

기본의미	① v. 덮다, 덮어 가리다(veil, overlay)
	② v. (어느 범위에) 걸치다, ~에 이르다, 망라하다(comprehend, include)
	③ n. 덮개, 뚜껑, 표지
TEPS 중요의미	④ v. (~의 거리를) 가다, 여행하다(travel, pass through)
	⑤ n. 은신처(shelter)
	⑥ v. 취재하다

critical

기본의미	① a. 비판적인(unfavorable, objective)
TEPS 중요의미	② a. 중요한(important, essential)
	③ a. 위독한(serious, dangerous)

cross

기본의미	① v. 지나가다(pass over)
	② v. 건너다(go across)
	③ v. 교차하다, 엇갈리다(intersect)
	④ n. 십자가, 십자형(cruciform)
TEPS 중요의미	⑤ v. 지우다(remove, erase)
	⑥ v. 포개다(put one upon another)
	⑦ a. 심술궂은(bad-tempered)
	⑧ a. 화난(angry)

cut

기본의미	① v. 베다, 자르다
TEPS 중요의미	② v. (인원이나 비용 등을) 삭감하다
	③ v. (계약 등의 일을) 하다

deliver

기본의미	① v. 배달하다, 전하다(bring, carry)
	② v. 연설하다, 설교하다, 선언하다, 발표하다(declare, announce)

TEPS 중요의미	③ v. 낳다(give birth to)
	④ v. (아이를) 낳다, 분만하다
	⑤ v. ~을 해방시키다; 구하다(set free, save, rescue)

due

기본의미	① a. 예정된
	② a. 때문에(due to)
TEPS 중요의미	③ a. 적절한

face

기본의미	① n. 얼굴
TEPS 중요의미	② n. 액면
	③ v. 직면하다

flat

기본의미	① a. 평평한, 평탄한, 수평의(even, level, horizontal)
	② a. 흥미 없는, 따분한, 시시한, 지루한, 단조로운(uninteresting, dull)
	③ a. 맛없는, 김빠진(untasty, favorless)
TEPS 중요의미	④ a. 공기가 빠진(not containing enough air, empty)
	⑤ a. 충전이 다 된
	⑥ a. 단호한
	⑦ n. 아파트

miss

기본의미	① v. 놓치다
TEPS 중요의미	② v. (장면 등을) 보지 못하다
	③ v. 그리워하다
	④ v. 빠지다

다의어

odd

기본의미
① a. 홀수의
② n. 홀수(an odd number)
③ a. 한 짝의
④ a. 남짓의(above, over, upward of)

TEPS 중요의미
⑤ a. 이상한(strange, unusual)
⑥ a. 임시의
⑦ v. 임시 일을 하다(do odd jobs)

passage

기본의미
① n. 통로, 복도, 좁은 길(corridor, hall)

TEPS 중요의미
② n. 통행, 통과(passing, going through)
③ n. (인용한) 일절(一節), 한 구절, (음악의) 악절

pose

기본의미
① v. 자세를 취하다
② v. 제출하다

TEPS 중요의미
③ v. 부과하다, 가하다
④ v. 내포하다

principal

기본의미
① a. 주요한, 중요한

TEPS 중요의미
② n. 교장
③ n. 주범

save

기본의미
① v. 저장하다
② v. 저금하다

TEPS 중요의미
③ v. (컴퓨터 파일을) 저장하다
④ v. 구하다

subject

기본의미
① n. 과목
② n. 주제(topic), 문제
③ n. 대상(target)

TEPS 중요의미
④ a. ~을 받기 쉬운, ~되기 쉬운
⑤ a. 지배받는
⑥ v. 예속시키다
⑦ v. 명령하다
⑧ v. 당하게 하다
⑨ n. 원인, 불평의 원인(subject of complaint)

turn

기본의미
① v. 회전하다
② n. 차례

TEPS 중요의미
③ n. 병의 발작
④ n. 재능

wave

기본의미
① n. 파도, 물결

TEPS 중요의미
② n. 곱슬머리
③ v. 손을 흔들다

wear

기본의미
① v. 입다(입고 있는 상태를 말함)
○ 오답 피하기 '입는 동작'을 말하는 put on과 혼동하지 않도록 주의
② v. 쇠약해지게 하다

TEPS 중요의미
③ v. (향수를) 뿌리다, (화장을) 하다(향수를 뿌린 상태나 화장을 한 상태를 말함)
○ 오답 피하기 '향수를 뿌리거나 화장을 하고 있는 동작'을 말하는 put on과 혼동하지 않도록 주의
④ v. 간직하다
⑤ v. 받아들이다
⑥ v. 오래 있으면서 폐를 끼치다(wear out one's welcome)

A. 다음 중 우리말에 적절한 어휘를 골라 체크하세요.

1. common ☐ practice 보편적인 관행
    ☐ exercise

2. ☐ position a wish 바램을 내포하다
    ☐ pose

3. ☐ wave good-bye 작별하다
    ☐ talk

4. ☐ put a perfume 향수를 뿌리다(상태)
    ☐ wear

B. 밑줄 친 어휘가 문장에서 어떤 의미로 쓰이고 있는지 써보세요.

5. This violin concerto was <u>arranged</u> for the piano by an American composer in 1935.

6. The old lady was really <u>cross</u> when the boy's ball broke the window.

7. Doing it that way, you will <u>contract</u> debts from everyone near you.

5. 이 바이올린 협주곡은 1935년에 한 미국 작곡가에 의해 피아노를 위한 곡으로 편곡되었다.

6. 소년의 공이 유리창을 깼을 때 그 노부인은 정말로 화가 났다.

7. 일을 그런 식으로 하면, 너는 주변의 모든 사람들에게 빚을 지게 될 것이다.

Answers

1. practice
2. pose
3. wave
4. wear
5. 편곡하다
6. 화가 난
7. 빚을 지다

★ Real Test_ 해당 범위 연습문제

Choose the best word for the blank.

1. A: A free hotel room for one week in Hawaii? What's the __________?
   B: You have to buy the airline tickets to Hawaii at the regular price.
   (a) catch
   (b) condition
   (c) order
   (d) case

2. A: It was us who really made this program a success.
   B: Give credit where credit is __________. Tom's help was indispensable, you know.
   (a) fine
   (b) worth
   (c) due
   (d) proper

3. Participating in the marathon will not only feel great, but you will be doing it for a
   good __________.
   (a) reason
   (b) cause
   (c) doubt
   (d) idea

4. On no __________ are you to touch an electric appliance with wet hands.
   (a) account
   (b) reason
   (c) explanation
   (d) experiment

5. The stress and fatigue from the hard work in the factory __________ seriously on the
   employees.
   (a) gear
   (b) wear
   (c) fear
   (d) rear

★**Random Test** _ 모든 범위의 연습문제

Choose the best word for the blank.

6. A: Which one is your brother Sam?
B: He is the one ___________ near the statues.
(a) lingering
(b) rallying
(c) deranging
(d) suffocate

7. A: Paul, it is dangerous to ride a bicycle when there is no bike __________.
B: I know. But I am always careful.
(a) lane
(b) line
(c) row
(d) passage

8. A: Jane said that she does not feel like going to school.
B: Why? Is she being ___________ by her classmates?
(a) bullied
(b) scared
(c) tolerated
(d) banned

9. A: I'm tired. Would you __________ the table for us?
B: So am I. How about ordering a pizza?
(a) fix
(b) arrange
(c) set
(d) do

10. A: Our son refuses to study and hangs out with his friends all night.
B: Don't worry. I think it's just a ___________ which teens usually experience.
(a) phase
(b) step
(c) scala
(d) phenomena

11. If you borrow that sort of money from the bank, the ____________ payments will be too high.
(a) minimal
(b) temporary
(c) instrumental
(d) governmental

12. As most great companies will tell you, effective communication is ____________ in order to succeed.
(a) critical
(b) dangerous
(c) vigilant
(d) disparaging

13. In some parts of the world, wild ____________ is eaten on a daily basis.
(a) game
(b) meal
(c) food
(d) clam

14. As more data became available to the public, opposition to the new dam gained ____________.
(a) moderation
(b) monopoly
(c) mobility
(d) momentum

15. The ruling party won the election by a ____________. Most people supported them.
(a) landslide
(b) earthquake
(c) avalanche
(d) seismology

Section Switch 

The issue of automobile safety looms ever larger. And now that industry has finally acceded to emission standards set years ago, the threat of global warming is pointing the finger at another villain; carbon dioxide, an enemy no catalytic converter can vanquish.

Translation

자동차 안전 문제는 그 어느 때보다 더욱 크게 부각되고 있다. 그리고 이제 자동차 업계는 수년 전에 제정된 배기가스 배출 기준에 마침내 동의했기 때문에 지구 온난화 현상의 위협은 또 다른 악역, 즉 자동차의 배기가스 정화 장치로도 이길 수 없는 적인 이산화탄소를 지목하고 있다.

Vocabulary

loom large 큰 문제로 다가오다, 크게 부각되다
accede to (처음에 반대했던 일에) 동의하다
emission standards 배기가스 배출 기준
threat 위협
global warming 지구 온난화 현상
point the finger at ~를 비난하다, ~의 잘못으로 지목하다
villain 악당, 악역
carbon dioxide 이산화탄소(CO_2)
catalytic converter 촉매 변환기(자동차의 배기가스 정화 장치)
vanquish ~를 제압하다, 이기다

Final Test

지금까지 650 돌파를 위해 꼭 필요한 어휘 및 표현들을 익혔다. 자,
이제 실전과 똑같은 유형의 어휘 영역 문제 50문항을 풀어보면서
앞서 익힌 어휘 및 표현을 실전에서 능숙하게 활용할 수 있는 감각
을 키워보도록 하자.

처음 문제를 풀 때는 반드시 실전과 똑같이 제한 시간 15분을 지켜
풀도록 해야 한다. 그런 다음, 〈정답 및 해설〉을 보며 틀린 문제는
두 번 다시 틀리지 않을 수 있도록 꼼꼼히 점검해두자. 맞힌 문제
역시 문제 속에 등장한 어휘나 표현 가운데 알지 못 했던 것은 반드
시 그 의미를 파악해 둔다. 이런 식으로 문제를 검토하는 과정에서
이미 알고 있던 어휘는 더욱 확실히 자기 것으로 만들 수 있고, 새
로운 어휘나 표현도 덤으로 익힐 수 있게 된다.

Choose the most appropriate word or expression for the blank in the conversation.

1. A: My father was __________ set against my choice.
    B: Then, how did you persuade him?
    (a) stand
    (b) opinion
    (c) dead
    (d) intention

2. A: I would like to invite you to dinner tonight.
    B: Can you give me a __________ check?
    (a) time
    (b) spare
    (c) rain
    (d) hit

3. A: What happened to you? Your trousers are __________ with mud.
    B: I slipped on an orange peel.
    (a) mixed
    (b) plastered
    (c) colored
    (d) centered

4. A: I am so disappointed. You could have done better than this.
    B: Well, I just don't get it. Why don't you __________ it out for me?
    (a) tell
    (b) explain
    (c) say
    (d) point

5. A: It is hard to make up my mind!
    B: Make the decision! Shape up or __________ out!
    (a) stand
    (b) bare
    (c) figure
    (d) ship

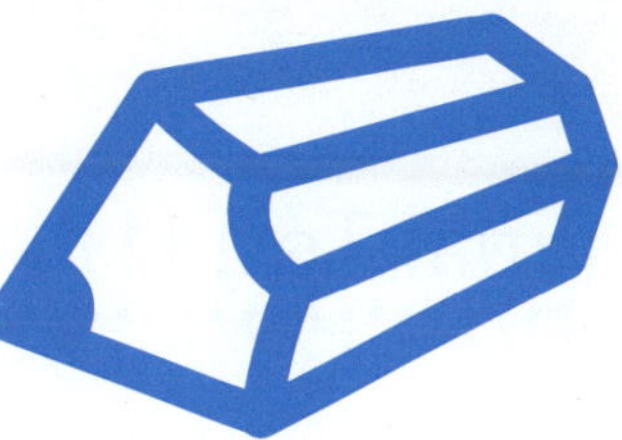

6. A: I seldom go out to eat.
    B: Neither do I. I go out to eat once in a __________.
    (a) cream cake
    (b) blue moon
    (c) piece of cake
    (d) habitual

7. A: I think history should be more than just an annalistic record of the past.
    B: I agree. Some __________ judgment is inevitable in the ordering and interpretation
      of events.
    (a) decadent
    (b) childish
    (c) subjective
    (d) historical

8. A: He has no means of support upon which to __________.
    B: Why doesn't he get a job?
    (a) receive
    (b) depend
    (c) carry
    (d) work

9. A: Can I borrow your cell phone? My battery is __________.
    B: Sure. Help yourself.
    (a) free
    (b) flat
    (c) vacant
    (d) fiery

10. A: Tom spent his vacation in Paris sick in bed in the hotel.
    B: That's the way the ball __________. I'm sure he must have been very disappointed.
    (a) bounces
    (b) flies
    (c) hops
    (d) jumps

Final Test (1)

11. A: It has happened already.
B: I know but I can't simply __________ my worries to rest.
(a) take
(b) need
(c) make
(d) put

12. A: What did Bob do when he saw the accident?
B: He was cool, calm and __________. He helped the injured and called the police.
(a) fresh
(b) serene
(c) collected
(d) tranquil

13. A: Isn't it too rude knocking on his door at this unholy hour?
B: Do you think it's too __________? Should we wait untill the morning?
(a) late
(b) early
(c) delayed
(d) postponed

14. A: Jane told me the other day that Larry lost his job.
B: He couldn't __________ the mustard, so they fired him.
(a) slice
(b) give
(c) promise
(d) cut

15. A: Peace and development are not so different as we may think them to be.
B: If it is true, they are two sides of the same coin. One cannot __________ without the other.
(a) produce
(b) process
(c) prospect
(d) progress

16. A: Both Marx and Simmel viewed the conflict as a pervasive and inevitable feature of
the social system.

B: I can agree that, but their ___________ intellectual purposes as well as their
assumptions about the nature of society are vastly different.

(a) respective
(b) respectable
(c) respectful
(d) respected

17. A: Thanks for the free pizza. Could I have a free cola, too?

B: Don't ___________ your luck.

(a) squeeze
(b) press
(c) harass
(d) use

18. A: It suits you perfectly. Buy it!

B: I wish I could but I just can't ___________ it.

(a) spend
(b) afford
(c) waste
(d) trouble

19. A: I take after my farther more than I do my mother. What about you?

B: I ___________ no resemblance to either of my parents.

(a) pay
(b) bear
(c) need
(d) tell

20. A: Honey, can you give me something casual to wear? This is too formal.

B: You are going to a ___________ dinner tonight, aren't you?

(a) black-tie
(b) fantastic
(c) stone
(d) casual

Final Test (1)

21. A: Young people today are wearing the same styles we wore in the 1960's.
B: As they say, history __________ itself.
(a) repeats
(b) calls
(c) returns
(d) questions

22. A: Don't even try to run away by yourself. Remember, we are on the same __________.
B: Stop nagging me, I know where I am.
(a) plane
(b) boat
(c) bus
(d) truck

23. A: Do you think he would resign?
B: Well, I don't think he would easily give up that __________ position.
(a) difficult
(b) catch
(c) cushy
(d) cushion

24. A: Don't even give him a single drop of alcohol.
B: I know, he is a __________ drinker.
(a) compulsive
(b) comprehensive
(c) complimental
(d) head

25. A: We could turn Mars into a paradise. The atmosphere needs to change and ironically,
pollution is the __________ which it needs.
B: I don't think that polluting Mars would be a big problem. We are doing that here on
earth.
(a) dirties
(b) dump
(c) medicine
(d) diseases

Choose the most appropriate word or expression for the blank in the statement.

26. Every living thing on Earth shares a long, colorful history. Our planet was born into a maelstrom 4.5 billion years ago, and for the next 600 million years a steady bombardment of primordial debris made the surface __________.
    (a) uninhabitable
    (b) breathable
    (c) peaceful
    (d) questionable

27. Sources say police had __________ considerable material over the past 10 days.
    (a) raised
    (b) accumulated
    (c) intented
    (d) illustrated

28. The 2004 amendments allow police to ask a magistrate to grant them "dead time", which stops the __________ while they check their information.
    (a) TV
    (b) surveillance
    (c) clock
    (d) computer

29. The extended detention period has been criticised by the Law Council and civil libertarians for being an __________ of anti-terrorist powers.
    (a) consideration
    (b) abuse
    (c) consensus
    (d) contention

30. To rectify the problem, police are __________ up the rules on illegal parking in this area.
    (a) tightening
    (b) suppressing
    (c) stirring
    (d) exerting

31. Each crew member has their own set of toiletries. Crew members also have individual urine funnels which are attached to hoses, which allows the urine to be __________ into a wastewater tank.
(a) matured
(b) deposited
(c) cleaned
(d) contained

32. What further differentiates humans from apes is the place where the spine __________ to the hips.
(a) subscribes
(b) attaches
(c) inclines
(d) treats

33. From the days of the founding fathers right on through the industrial revolution and two world wars, Americans literally __________ over other nations.
(a) measured
(b) jumped
(c) towered
(d) talented

34. In order to stay stress free, it's important that we have some time for __________. It helps us to clear out minds and begin a new day.
(a) reflection
(b) refraction
(c) deflation
(d) refraction

35. James is famous with his __________ skills. But today's crab dish was really awful.
(a) cook
(b) culinary
(c) main dish
(d) crap

36. Due to the political conspiracy, the Democratic party insisted that __________ should be directed towards the Clinton government.
    (a) liability
    (b) vindication
    (c) impediment
    (d) corrodibility

37. In order to win the election, they __________ a range of tactics.
    (a) have
    (b) hunted
    (c) employed
    (d) possessed

38. Unlike American firms, which seek a balanced relationship with regional law firms, British firms employ a full-fledge approach and seek to __________ local firms.
    (a) oversee
    (b) dominate
    (c) master
    (d) command

39. Nothing will rekindle the __________ unless there is a breach of contract.
    (a) signs
    (b) stories
    (c) reasons
    (d) debates

40. John was __________ when she told him that even though he was stupid and lazy, he would always be her best friend.
    (a) incensed
    (b) stimulated
    (c) enraptured
    (d) invigorated

41. _________ is pervasive in our society, and Christians need to know how to combat these teachings and how to challenge atheists to rethink their beliefs.
(a) Creationism
(b) Darwinism
(c) Saintism
(d) Citycism

42. Rice and Gheit discussed topics of _________ interest to the United States and Egypt.
(a) mutual
(b) ambiguous
(c) vague
(d) good

43. As you _________ your skin directly to Sun frequently, the possibility of skin cancer increases.
(a) expose
(b) disclose
(c) produce
(d) display

44. The final destination where we need to advance this _________ tonight is Inchon.
(a) meeting
(b) conference
(c) association
(d) operation

45. They all agreed that the _________ of the corrupt corporation was chaos, bankruptcy and despair.
(a) penance
(b) request
(c) legacy
(d) punishment

46. ELS is an environmental problem-solving team __________ to offering the highest quality solutions that meet the environmental demands of today and tomorrow.
(a) dedicated
(b) worked
(c) maintained
(d) operated

47. We are __________ to increasing the financial strength of the company and to provide dependability for our clients and career opportunities for current and future employees.
(a) committed
(b) mitigated
(c) creolized
(d) pleased

48. The part of the Milky Way in the __________ of the south celestial pole is either out of sight or else it never rises high enough for a favorable view from the United States.
(a) vicinity
(b) reflection
(c) alternative
(d) supplement

49. Although many people have a bad reaction to certain foods, a true food allergy is a reaction __________ by the immune system.
(a) used
(b) diseased
(c) maintained
(d) triggered

50. Beijing made some __________, namely offering to enlarge the 800-strong election committee charged with selecting a new leader. However, opposition leaders say the proposals do not go far enough.
(a) concessions
(b) projects
(c) allowances
(d) agreements

Choose the most appropriate word or expression for the blank in the conversation.

1. A: I broke up with my boyfriend. Now I'm a ___________ woman.
   B: That's too bad. I thought he was a nice guy.
   (a) ample
   (b) single
   (c) continued
   (d) sent

2. A: I heard that they died in the a car accident. What happened?
   B: The cars caught fire on impact and they were __________.
   (a) extinguished
   (b) incinerated
   (c) executed
   (d) discarded

3. A: Dad! This rock has a very strange shape.
   B: I guess it has been ___________ by water from this ceiling.
   (a) melted
   (b) cut
   (c) dissolved
   (d) eroded

4. A: Do you know the meaning of "So help you God," when used at a trial?
   B: I think so. "So help you God" could be __________ as "Let God help you do so".
   (a) composited
   (b) prosed
   (c) articled
   (d) paraphrased

5. A: What is the main reason why we need to withdraw the product from that market?
   B: Basically, the defense market in Korea has become too small to sustain economically
      viable production __________.
   (a) names
   (b) brands
   (c) runs
   (d) hands

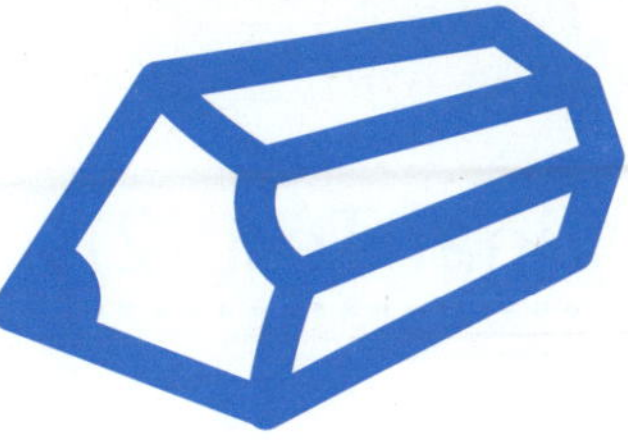

6. A: How do you spell "committee?"

B: I'm not sure. I will __________ for you . Here it is. It has two m's, two t's and two e's.

(a) take it up

(b) look it up

(c) get it up

(d) pull it up

7. A: She did whatever she could do to make herself look better.

B: I know. She even had __________ to change the shape of her nose.

(a) pharyngeal surgery

(b) hemorrhoidectomy

(c) plastic surgery

(d) kidney transplant

8. A: So, you have good marks! That's amazing news. You didn't study for the exam until I arrived at your house.

B: Yes, that's true. But I was __________ for the exam just a few days before.

(a) studying

(b) cramming

(c) preparing

(d) peering

9. A: Robert and Sam share an intensely selfish, __________ nature.

B: I totally agree with you.

(a) egotistic

(b) grilled

(c) arrogant

(d) elegant

10. A: The competition was very difficult. But Sam eventually __________ it off and won first prize.

B: That's great news!

(a) turned

(b) gave

(c) pulled

(d) missed

11. A: You cheated, because your tennis racket is bigger than mine!
B: Don't be such a _________ loser. It's only a game.
(a) painful
(b) tender
(c) sensitive
(d) sore

12. A: Doctor Jones _________ your scars when you were injured?
B: Yes. He took good care of me.
(a) cured
(b) received
(c) treated
(d) offered

13. A: Look at the sun. It's _________.
B: Here, put some sun block on. This is extra strong.
(a) primitive
(b) heat
(c) a furnace
(d) taciturn

14. A: You do the work first and then we'll discuss your pay.
B: Come on, I wasn't born _________.
(a) Monday
(b) yesterday
(c) last year
(d) Sunday

15. A: The flat has been _________ cleaned.
B: Already? It was such a mess.
(a) debonairly
(b) putridly
(c) determinately
(d) meticulously

16. A: Should we consider employing this job applicant?
B: I'm not too sure. He's __________. He was jailed for 5 years.
(a) a black man
(b) an ex-convict
(c) an ex-worker
(d) a fund manager

17. A: Do you want to pass the University entrance exam? Study hard!
B: Of course I do. But, all work and no play makes Jack a __________ boy.
(a) clever
(b) dummy
(c) dull
(d) disable

18. A: Last night I __________ that I won Lotto.
B: Really? What were the winning numbers?
(a) lulled
(b) sleeked
(c) peered
(d) dreamed

19. A: Your answer was not even close! I think it was just a __________ in the dark!
B: What was the correct answer?
(a) knock
(b) whistle
(c) sing a song
(d) tune off

20. A: The antique shop owner said that the painting was very rare. He couldn't even say how much it is worth.
B: Oh, then it must be __________.
(a) valueless
(b) priceless
(c) costless
(d) accountable

Final Test (2)

21. A: I'm going to use my bonus on a trip to Mexico.
   B: You ought to save a little for a __________ day.
   (a) late
   (b) dark
   (c) rainy
   (d) difficult

22. A: Jenny won the $15,000 scholarship.
   B: I knew she could do it. She has always been such a __________ student.
   (a) volatile
   (b) fraternal
   (c) tenacious
   (d) dull

23. A: Just stop it! I won't __________ up with your lies anymore.
   B: But I'm telling you the truth.
   (a) be patient
   (b) stand
   (c) put
   (d) endure

24. A: Sonny took seriously what I meant for a joke.
   B: He is very much __________ to such a joke.
   (a) scrupulous
   (b) susceptible
   (c) insufficient
   (d) inadequate

25. A: What should we do if they invite us to dinner?
   B: I don't know. Let's just play it by __________.
   (a) ear
   (b) hair
   (c) eyes
   (d) listening

Choose the most appropriate word or expression for the blank in the statement.

26. If your friends and family get fat, chances are you will too. This conclusion was reached by researchers in a startling new study that suggests that __________ is socially contagious, and can spread easily from person to person.
    (a) obesity
    (b) disease
    (c) pollution
    (d) contamination

27. Britain banned the export of __________ products and halted the movement of cattle, sheep, goats and pigs across the country.
    (a) animals
    (b) wilds
    (c) livestock
    (d) cows

28. The officials, who spoke on condition of __________ because they weren't authorized to release the information, said another clash erupted about three hours later in Karbala.
    (a) secret
    (b) animosity
    (c) confidential
    (d) anonymity

29. To small children, the belly button, also known as the __________ or umbilicus, is one of the great mysteries of life.
    (a) navel
    (b) spine
    (c) tail
    (d) middle spot

30. A Hawaiian man was hospitalized with symptoms of __________ poisoning after eating canned chili that was subject to the recall.
    (a) botulism
    (b) malnutrition
    (c) epidemic
    (d) diabetes

31. Walt Disney Co. on Wednesday became the first major Hollywood studio to ban _________ of smoking, saying that there would be no smoking in its family-oriented movies.
(a) explanations
(b) depictions
(c) elucidations
(d) expositions

32. The probes found that nine officers were at fault in providing false information and that they should be held _________.
(a) searchable
(b) conductible
(c) amicable
(d) accountable

33. The study _________ that "boredom" was the main reason why so many people hate their job.
(a) condemned
(b) criticized
(c) varied
(d) specified

34. Indonesian doctors are investigating the _________ of an unknown illness that has killed eight people and infected 22 in a Java village.
(a) contamination
(b) disease
(c) outbreak
(d) entrance

35. Though women are employed in every part of Korea's labor force, the leadership roles in politics have been off _________ to them until recently.
(a) limits
(b) obstacles
(c) ends
(d) filters

36. It is also "plausible" that "areas of the brain which correspond to actions such as eating food may be __________ if these actions are observed by others."
(a) seen
(b) realized
(c) stimulated
(d) accessed

37. Police in China seized one ton of fake Viagra pills during a series of raids on gangs that were making __________ drugs to sell domestically and overseas.
(a) eatable
(b) counterfeit
(c) effective
(d) pharmaceutical

38. Schools in the __________ nation, which ironically brought the world the adult books, have shied away from educating youngsters about such topics as human reproduction.
(a) opened
(b) conservative
(c) progressive
(d) meticulous

39. __________ billowed into the sky and fires burned on the ground after the thunderous explosion.
(a) missile
(b) smoke
(c) weapons
(d) bullets

40. With the American public's patience wearing __________, many in Congress are pressing for a troop reduction.
(a) tough
(b) thick
(c) thin
(d) mutual

41. San Francisco's mayor banned city employees from using city funds to buy bottled water when __________ water is available.
(a) subterranean
(b) pond
(c) plumb
(d) tap

42. It showed that women are more __________ to drugs than men as 48.5 percent of the women respondents said they take drugs on a regular basis while only 34.4 percent of men reported doing so.
(a) vulnerable
(b) addicted
(c) favourable
(d) inevitable

43. Hundreds of demonstrators clashed with security forces outside the mosque and occupied it for several hours before being __________.
(a) reached
(b) removed
(c) dispersed
(d) arrived

44. Indian soldiers and civil rescue teams remain on standby in north-eastern Assam state as flash floods __________ by heavy monsoon rains displaced 600,000 people.
(a) flourished
(b) triggered
(c) missed
(d) waved

45. Four Russian diplomats expelled from Britain in a __________ over Moscow's refusal to extradite the murder suspect in the Litvinenko affair have left the country.
(a) stand-out
(b) stand-off
(c) stand-down
(d) stand-up

46. In the absence of the Chair and VC, the director shall __________ the duties and responsibilities of both.
(a) replace
(b) assume
(c) create
(d) constitute

47. A gunman who __________ with a huge sum of money from a local casino is still on the run Friday morning.
(a) used on
(b) made off
(c) put off
(d) paid on

48. Russian Czar Nicholas II, who was __________ in 1917 as a revolutionary fervor swept Russia, was eventually detained.
(a) abdicated
(b) inaugurated
(c) fired
(d) stepped

49. The report dealt with alcohol consumption by astronauts. The findings suggest that two of them were __________.
(a) tensed
(b) added
(c) excited
(d) intoxicated

50. A Cape Cod man who claimed he was homophobic, racist and a habitual liar to avoid jury duty earned an angry rebuke from a __________, who referred the case to prosecutors for possible charges.
(a) police
(b) black man
(c) homosexual
(d) judge

Choose the most appropriate word or expression for the blank in the conversation.

1. A: Laser lights are dangerous. You can make a person __________ blind with those.
   B: Don't worry. I won't point it at anyone's eyes.
   (a) have
   (b) go
   (c) be
   (d) see

2. A: I don't know why, but everything I have done so far today has been a disaster.
   B: Maybe you got up on the wrong side of the __________ this morning.
   (a) cradle
   (b) bed
   (c) layer
   (d) way

3. A: Did your mother get angry when she saw your report card?
   B: Yes, she blew a __________.
   (a) fuse
   (b) fuss
   (c) care
   (d) jack

4. A: I am calling about the secretarial position advertised in classified ads.
   B: Oh, sorry. It's already been __________.
   (a) filled
   (b) possessed
   (c) applied
   (d) taken

5. A: My brother got __________ A's in his finals.
   B: I'm not at all surprised. He is such a diligent student.
   (a) all
   (b) straight
   (c) full
   (d) serial

6. A: You should let her do that job by herself. She'll be offended if you try to help.
B: I know. I certainly don't want to __________ on her toes.
(a) block
(b) room
(c) ladder
(d) step

7. A: I think I've burnt my __________. I told her that I'm seeing someone else.
B: I don't think that was a good move.
(a) line
(b) mountain
(c) house
(d) bridges

8. A: I would really like to go on a date with Amanda.
B: Well, try and __________ favor with her.
(a) curry
(b) take
(c) hamper
(d) shield

9. A: If you want to be a sales manager, you should be good at __________ a hard bargain.
B: Thank you for your advice, Dad.
(a) driving
(b) dropping
(c) carrying
(d) managing

10. A: How was your vacation?
B: It was great. I really went to __________ at the casino. I won $500.
(a) town
(b) pub
(c) city
(d) downtown

11. A: We'll have to work on these reports all night.
   B: Then, we may as well __________ some coffee.
   (a) brew
   (b) broil
   (c) brand
   (d) breed

12. A: We need to catch hold of this man as soon as possible.
   B: Sorry, sir. But we do not have the slightest __________ about his whereabouts.
   (a) glue
   (b) clue
   (c) blue
   (d) slew

13. A: I have a painful __________ in my foot.
   B: That's too bad. You will not be able to walk for another week.
   (a) swelling
   (b) spelling
   (c) clearing
   (d) steering

14. A: I never knew that he was an adopted child.
   B: Yes. The poor boy has never known his __________ parents.
   (a) chemical
   (b) biological
   (c) regional
   (d) political

15. A: It's surprising that the insurgents suddenly laid down their arms before the government.
   B: I don't think so. There is a rumor around that both parties have signed a secret deal which is all __________ in mystery.
   (a) oaked
   (b) stoked
   (c) soaked
   (d) cloaked

16. A: The university has given me _______ scholarship which only covers the fees of the course.
   B: Then, who will pay for the rest of your expenses?
   (a) full
   (b) educational
   (c) partial
   (d) travel

17. A: This bill presented by the government is completely against the constitution.
   B: Yes, but the government can always use its majority power to __________ the constitution and pass this bill in the parliament.
   (a) mend
   (b) amend
   (c) end
   (d) send

18. A: Do you remember those evenings when we used to walk together along the riverside in the forest?
   B: Sure I do. I still __________ the memory of those good old days I spent with you.
   (a) cherish
   (b) nourish
   (c) wish
   (d) think

19. A: It's no use complaining to him. He has no control over his own team.
   B: That's why people say he is a ___________.
   (a) professional
   (b) spent force
   (c) good manager
   (d) wise man

20. A: This is the second time that I have not been selected for the national team.
   B: You don't have to be upset about it as you can still try again and you are still allowed to coach the juniors. You should also look on the __________ side and be positive about the future.
   (a) right
   (b) dark
   (c) light
   (d) bright

Final Test (3)

21. A: I will call this gathering a __________ meeting.
   B: Indeed, I agree with you as all of us have finally agreed to have a common policy
      that addresses the different issues we have raised.
   (a) breakthrough
   (b) breakpoint
   (c) break-up
   (d) break time

22. A: Do you know the cause of death of this person?
   B: Not yet, sir. The doctors are yet to __________ the autopsy.
   (a) treat
   (b) perform
   (c) recover
   (d) operate

23. A: He was so depressed about losing all of his money that he killed himself..
   B: I think he must have been __________ of all hope and support.
   (a) slept
   (b) swept
   (c) bereft
   (d) dwelt

24. A: Are you planning to buy a new car?
   B: No. I just bought a new house so I can't __________ a car. Perhaps next year.
   (a) drive
   (b) afford
   (c) repair
   (d) exchange

25. A: The Chinese philosopher, Lao Tzu wrote a book titled "Tao Te Ching." It's the most
      __________ book I have ever read. Have you read it?
   B: Yes. It's like understanding and not understanding at the same time. In other words,
      it's like reading but not reading the book.
   (a) paradoxical
   (b) heavy
   (c) lengthy
   (d) short

Choose the most appropriate word or expression for the blank in the statement.

26. Family violence and neglect has often gone unreported. Societies attitude towards such failing often makes ___________ violence an issue which is rarely discussed.
(a) patrimonial
(b) juvenile
(c) counterfeit
(d) conjugal

27. Even though their village was completely destroyed by a flood, the villagers showed no sign of __________ and rebuilt their new village within a month.
(a) boredom
(b) courage
(c) despair
(d) flexibility

28. He was initially an honest guy. But before long, his ___________ behavior had become a problem.
(a) insidious
(b) steadfast
(c) treacherous
(d) scrupulous

29. Surrounded by a host of besiegers and unable to replenish their supplies, the defenders of the castle feared their food would soon be __________.
(a) exhausted
(b) hoarded
(c) superfluous
(d) obtainable

30. Their married life was not cogent since it was often __________ with bitter fighting and arguments.
(a) imminent
(b) fraught
(c) obvious
(d) tranquil

31. She was pleased by the accolades she received; like everyone else, she enjoyed being

__________.

(a) praised
(b) playful
(c) entertained
(d) vindicated

32. It took him a long time to come to __________ with the fact that he was never going to be a great author.
(a) acceptance
(b) understanding
(c) allowances
(d) terms

33. He had taken a pair of white rats into the church and had let them __________ on the floor.
(a) tight
(b) dead
(c) careless
(d) loose

34. Because they are held accountable by the public, politicians have a __________ interest in insulating themselves against scandal.
(a) settled
(b) provoked
(c) restricted
(d) vested

35. Heavy income taxes, which exert a stranglehold on the economy, have __________ sources of new investment capital.
(a) swallowed up
(b) crippled
(c) choked off
(d) tied up

36. These remarks indicate that you are __________ and unaware of life's realities.
   (a) clever
   (b) stimulating
   (c) wily
   (d) ingenuous

37. Good sportsmanship requires you to accept the umpire's decision, even if you do not __________ with it.
   (a) concur
   (b) deny
   (c) protest
   (d) catch up

38. Though polio has been practically wiped out, there have been __________ cases of the disease.
   (a) imminent
   (b) sporadic
   (c) commencing
   (d) frequent

39. The sewage will decay and the water will begin to __________ odors.
   (a) take hold of
   (b) succumb to
   (c) tell on
   (d) give off

40. The company was accused of selling milk that had been __________ by the addition of water.
   (a) condensed
   (b) improved
   (c) enriched
   (d) adulterated

41. Although he was a grown man with a family, he behaved __________, clamoring for attention if he did not get his way.
(a) infantile
(b) inoffensive
(c) eclectic
(d) estranged

42. My confidence in my ability to play the violin was really __________ when I failed to impress the audience at the last concert.
(a) undermined
(b) considered
(c) loosened
(d) sabotaged

43. The governor commented on the disadvantages of political __________, saying that after his extended tenure in office the voters had grown used to blaming him for everything.
(a) decorum
(b) debate
(c) belief
(d) longevity

44. Because of Eileen's sharp tongue and quick temper, it is __________ that her insulting remarks will provoke a fight.
(a) unusual
(b) incidental
(c) inevitable
(d) influential

45. Russia urged that oil __________ from a pipeline near Latvia contaminated the soil.
(a) leaking
(b) detaining
(c) slashing
(d) draining

46. He had realized the mistake he had made and wanted to __________ himself.
- (a) retain
- (b) retail
- (c) redeem
- (d) relished

47. More and more victims turn to litigation to __________ wrong done to them.
- (a) embrace
- (b) redress
- (c) sue
- (d) mark

48. The company went bankrupt last year. As a result, my husband was made __________.
- (a) unbounded
- (b) visitative
- (c) redundant
- (d) affirmative

49. Don't blame the airplane's ventilation system the next time you experience dry eyes and headaches while flying. It's the interaction between your oily body and ozone in the upper atmosphere that is the real __________.
- (a) culprit
- (b) reference
- (c) inference
- (d) mission

50. While the U.S. troops suffered from a shortage of provisions, the German troops seemed to have an __________ supply of ammunitions.
- (a) insufficient
- (b) deficient
- (c) inexhaustible
- (d) wanting

Choose the most appropriate word or expression for the blank in the conversation.

1. A: We have so little time to __________ lunch for all the participants.
    B: Don't worry. Not all of them will be eating here.
    (a) eat
    (b) repair
    (c) prepare
    (d) cook

2. A: What is the good news you wanted to tell me?
    B: I have now taken on the _______ of the company manager and have become your boss.
    (a) files
    (b) shoes
    (c) clothes
    (d) mantle

3. A: Thank God! You have come back safe and sound from the middle of the battlefield.
    B: Trust me. It was a __________ escape.
    (a) sorrow
    (b) shallow
    (c) narrow
    (d) hollow

4. A: Why are you bent upon resigning from this job?
    B: Because my boss has made my life __________ all the way.
    (a) miserable
    (b) misery
    (c) mystery
    (d) missing

5. A: I heard about this lady who was the first person to think of setting up a hospital for
       the rural people in this area.
    B: Not just that. She actually _________ the concept of establishing a cooperative clinic
       for rural people so that they could afford healthcare in these villages.
    (a) possessed
    (b) prayed
    (c) pioneered
    (d) played

6. A: Did you hear that? Everyone is talking about it. The boss is having an affair with
   the new secretary.
   B: Yes. That news is spreading like __________.
   (a) channels
   (b) media
   (c) wings
   (d) wildfire

7. A: In spite of inviting him to the party so many times, he did not come.
   B: You know, he does not mix with people. He is very __________.
   (a) unsatisfied
   (b) unsociable
   (c) unsorted
   (d) unselfish

8. A: Joe sent quite a few e-mails complaining about her boss. Then, somebody
   forwarded them to the boss.
   B: She's in hot __________ now!
   (a) water
   (b) fired
   (c) contradiction
   (d) potato

9. A: Look, I've got to get back home, I've got loads of studying to do.
   B: Oh relax! The books can wait. Tim's buying the next __________. What do you want
   to drink?
   (a) round
   (b) bill
   (c) treat
   (d) bottle

10. A: Oh, no. It's time to pay the rent again. Comes round fast enough, doesn't it?
   B: Yeah, and I'm so __________ right now. I don't know where my money goes.
   (a) miserable
   (b) impoverish
   (c) deprive
   (d) broke

Final Test (4)

11. A: I have my exam today. I should have re-read what I studied in the class. I'm really
worried.
B: It's important to __________ for exams but you went out every night this week.
(a) precautious
(b) preview
(c) devise
(d) revise

12. A: Wow, this is a great gift. How can I ever thank you Mr. Jones?
B: Well, you can start by dropping the __________. Please, call me Tom.
(a) formality
(b) courteous
(c) formalization
(d) hypocrisy

13. A: Well, I've been feeling sick ever since I had sushi a few days ago. My stomach's
still upset, and I feel dizzy.
B: I see. Any other __________?
(a) sentimental
(b) symptoms
(c) senses
(d) complaints

14. A: Can we go and look at the shoes now?
B: Yes, and after that I expect we'll all be feeling __________, so we'll go and grab a
bite to eat.
(a) peckish
(b) depressed
(c) exhausted
(d) soberly

15. A: What's up with you?
B: Well, I've just __________ on a part-time course here at the university, and I'm still a
student at the language school!
(a) registered
(b) enrolled
(c) applied
(d) filed

16. A: If you want to rent it to him, you'll have to give him a discount.

B: Well, I suppose I could let him have a small __________. But what am I supposed to say to other renters?

(a) deduction

(b) reduction

(c) thrifty

(d) augmentation

17. A: You're making some very serious __________. Do you actually have any hard evidence?

B: Well, I bet the police do. I bet it's only a matter of time before they arrest the criminal.

(a) allegations

(b) conviction

(c) fraud

(d) approval

18. A: Thank you so much. I was __________ a cheat, a liar and a thief, but because of you I'm beginning to clear my name.

B: It was nothing. The truth will come out, as they say.

(a) trapped

(b) committed

(c) branded

(d) honored

19. A: I've been __________ my studies and I want to get back on the right track.

B: Well, that is good news. What's brought on this change of heart?

(a) distracting

(b) devoting

(c) neglecting

(d) searching

20. A: Oh, he wasn't injured in that accident, then.

B: No. He is just a born __________. Luckily he was able to avoid being in the hospital by the accident.

(a) hurter

(b) injured

(c) cripple

(d) heater

21. A: Did you hear that Claire's house was robbed last night?

B: Really? I usually leave a light on in the house when I go out at night. I think it makes _________ think twice about breaking in.

(a) poachers

(b) burglars

(c) shoplifters

(d) smugglers

22. A: I'll go there. But it will be between 10 a.m. and 2 p.m.

B: Can you be more _________? I can't wait all day.

(a) specimen

(b) speculative

(c) special

(d) specific

23. A: I can't remember where I put my credit card when I left the restaurant.

B: You had better _________ it to the bank now.

(a) tell

(b) report

(c) appraise

(d) confirm

24. A: I'm afraid there is no one by that name in this department. You must have the _________ number.

B: Oh, I'm awfully sorry.

(a) wrong

(b) missed

(c) bad

(d) sinister

25. A: Did you _________ around before hiring a contractor?

B: Yes, I did. As a matter of fact, I got three estimates, and I went for the middle price.

(a) shop

(b) ask

(c) come

(d) hang

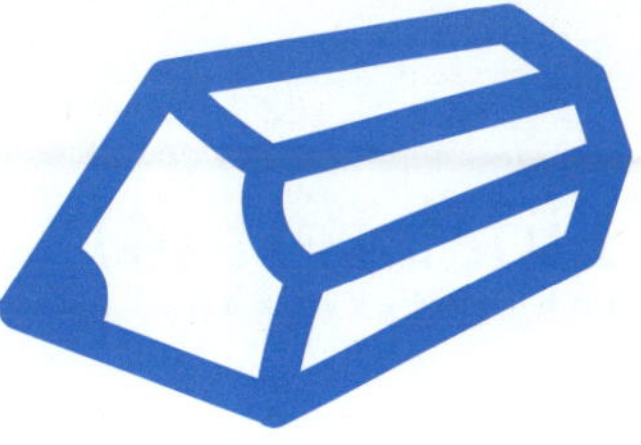

Choose the most appropriate word or expression for the blank in the statement.

26. The crisis was caused by the government's reckless decision _________ towards war. People fear what will happen in the near future but take it for granted.
    (a) interferingly
    (b) interestingly
    (c) inexorably
    (d) pursuantly

27. The offender could be imprisoned because the law says "_________ of the fire regulation is punishable by a fine or imprisonment."
    (a) obedience
    (b) confinement
    (c) infringement
    (d) submission

28. When we _________ a mineral it must be combined with an amino acid to be absorbed.
    (a) ingest
    (b) overeat
    (c) throw out
    (d) chew

29. The silver medal bears the sovereign's head and the _________ 'for distinguished service'
    (a) inscription
    (b) instruction
    (c) explanation
    (d) subtle

30. That a person or organization is _________ means that he or it does not have enough money to pay their debts.
    (a) abundant
    (b) insolvent
    (c) declaration
    (d) loanable

31. The violence over the last forty-eight hours was __________ by the ex-members of the secret police.
(a) instigated
(b) resulted
(c) trespassed
(d) infeasible

32. She had sent a letter to her husband in the prison. Her letter had been __________ by the Secret Service before he received it.
(a) intercepted
(b) delayed
(c) obstructed
(d) sealed

33. The Canadian government __________ a decade-old policy that required prospective Sikh immigrants to change their last names to avoid confusion with other Sikhs.
(a) passed
(b) nixed
(c) reversed
(d) objected

34. Some people claim that the government should __________ religious taxes on Christian commercial transactions. They also claim that these commercialized transactions are no longer religious matters.
(a) exempt
(b) immunize
(c) remit
(d) levy

35. Dve to the strong opposition to this bill, members of congress were warned of possible __________ if their vote went through.
(a) commencement
(b) deficiency
(c) repercussion
(d) causation

36. As the domestic market becomes __________, firms need to export their products.
(a) saturated
(b) abundant
(c) prevailed
(d) underage

37. The music industry will gradually abandon the manufacturing of unprofitable compact disks for more __________ mp3 players.
(a) simple
(b) lucrative
(c) streamlined
(d) futuristic

38. After the scouts returned, the general __________ down the location of the enemy camp.
(a) save
(b) pinned
(c) simmer
(d) come

39. If we __________ together, we still have a chance at winning.
(a) stiffen
(b) stick
(c) cement
(d) soften

40. The security camera company advertised the following: "Armed citizens __________ crime and save lives!"
(a) defer
(b) differ
(c) deter
(d) diffuse

Final Test (4)

41. To take a life through violence is a __________ crime, adequately punished by the death penalty.
(a) deleterious
(b) impudent
(c) hideous
(d) prudential

42. The current financial turmoil shows that most Asian economics are like high flying __________, dependent not on their own intrinsic strength but on the wind and the string.
(a) eagles
(b) kites
(c) airplanes
(d) rockets

43. Unlike ordinary parks, botanical gardens and __________ are laid out with more than just the beauty of the landscape in mind.
(a) arboretums
(b) auditorium
(c) conservatory
(d) oratorium

44. If you make a __________ of a charge that has been made against you, you make a statement which gives reasons why the accusation is untrue.
(a) retraction
(b) rebuttal
(c) compromise
(d) rebuke

45. Like the __________ performance, moreover, the sonata realizes its formative principle of excess in visual, as well as musical terms.
(a) virtuoso
(b) fiasco
(c) fresco
(d) painting

46. Steel is not as __________ as cast iron: it doesn't break as easily.
 (a) blunt
 (b) brisk
 (c) brilliant
 (d) brittle

47. The technology we have developed recently will give us the competitive __________ we need to maintain our profit trend.
 (a) strength
 (b) edge
 (c) reinforcement
 (d) advantage

48. __________' is the feeling some people experience when they travel to a new country or different part of the world for the first time.
 (a) Culture shock
 (b) Excitement
 (c) Curiosity
 (d) Melancholy feeling

49. I expressed my __________ at being unfairly dismissed at the audit.
 (a) indignation
 (b) sadness
 (c) happiness
 (d) gratitude

50. You have to remember that the education you receive will provide you with the knowledge necessary for the __________ of your goals.
 (a) development
 (b) establishment
 (c) attainment
 (d) amendment

정답 및 해설

Chapter 1 ~ 9의 Actual Test와 Final Test 4회분의 정답과 해설
이다. 틀린 문제는 두 번 다시 틀리지 않을 수 있도록 꼼꼼히 점검
해두되, 점검하는 과정에서 새롭게 등장한 어휘나 표현들도 반드시
익혀두도록 해야 한다. 맞힌 문제 역시 주어진 대화나 문장의 의미
를 제대로 파악하고 맞혔는지 해석을 보며 철저히 파악해두도록 한
다.

1.

해석_ A: 죄송해요, 차가 막혀서 늦었어요.

B: 난 더 이상 그렇게 판에 박힌 변명은 듣고 싶지 않아요.

해설_ lame excuse 뻔한 변명

어휘_ be held up in ~에 갇혀 꼼짝 못하다 dim 침침한

정답_ (a)

2.

해석_ A: 왜 집에 안 갔어?

B: 친구 전화 기다리고 있어.

해설_ 친구한테서 '전화가 오기로 되어 있어서 그 전화를 기다리고 있다' 고 할 때는 expecting을 쓴다.

어휘_ anticipate 기대하다

정답_ (c)

3.

해석_ 민주 사회에서, 더 많은 시민들이 유권자로서 그들의 힘을 행사해야 한다.

해설_ exercise는 권리 등을 '행사하다' 라는 의미를 가진다.

어휘_ voter 투표자 work out (문제 등을) 처리하다

정답_ (a)

4.

해석_ 서비스 개선 사업부에 불편 사항을 신고하려면 영수증과 보증서 사본이 전부 필요하다.

해설_ file a complaint 불만을 제기하다, 불편 사항을 신고하다

어휘_ warranty 보증서 nag 잔소리하다

정답_ (c)

5.

해석_ 그 휴전 협정에 따르면 비무장 지대를 제외하고 대인 지뢰의 사용을 금지하기로 규정하고 있다.

해설_ impose a ban 금지령을 내리다

어휘_ cease-fire 휴전 antipersonnel 대인 landmine 지뢰 demilitarize 비무장하다

정답_ (c)

6.

해석_ A: 공동 예금 계좌를 만들어 보는 것이 어때?

B: 그거 좋겠는데. 그러면 엄마랑 같이 쓸 수 있을 거야.

해설_ 공동 예금 계좌(joint account)의 의미가 되어야 B가 한 말과 내용상 합치된다.

어휘_ savings account 예금 계좌

정답_ (a)

7.

해석_ A: 주말 어땠니, Trent?

B: 끝내줬어! 대사관에서 호주의 독립 기념일을 축하하기 위해 성대한 파티를 열었어.

해설_ throw a party 파티를 열다

어휘_ embassy 대사관 celebrate 축하하다

정답_ (a)

8.

해석_ 나는 여러 가지 그의 논평을 두고 그와 대립했다. 나는 그의 논평들이 불공평하다고 생각했다.

해설_ take issue with ~와 대립하다, 논쟁하다

어휘_ offence 위반, 반칙

정답_ (c)

9.

해석_ 러시아 정부는 채무를 변제할 자금을 얻기 위한 협약을 성사시키기 위해 필사적으로 노력하고 있다.

해설_ work out 성사시키다, 성공시키다

어휘_ make up 만들다, 화장하다 hand over 전달하다 sign up 계약을 체결하다

정답_ (d)

10.

해석_ 이 비밀번호가 있으면 어떤 사람이라도 회사의 비밀 정보에 접근할 수 있다.

해설_ gain access to는 '접근하다' 의 의미로서 시설물이나 정보 등에의 접근을 말한다.

어휘_ confidential 비밀스러운 corporate information 회사(의) 정보 excess 초과

정답_ (a)

11.

해석_ 학생들은 불공정한 무역 관행에 항의하기 위해서 대사관 앞에서 데모를 하였다.

해설_ stage a demonstration 시위하다

어휘_ protest 항거하다, 항의하다 trade practice 무역 관행

정답_(c)

12.

해석_그녀의 뛰어난 생각들은 과학계에서 많은 주목을 받았다.

해설_draw attention은 '관심을 끌다, 주목을 받다' 라는 의미로 타당하다.

어휘_draw 끌다, 매혹하다 depend 의존하다 miss 놓치다, 그리워하다 proceed 전진하다

정답_(a)

13.

해석_컴퓨터 바이러스는 데이터를 즉시 파괴하거나 잠복해 있다가 나중에 피해를 입힐 수 있다.

해설_'피해를 주다' 는 do damage를 쓴다.

어휘_right away 즉시 lie dormant 잠복해 있다

정답_(b)

14.

해석_협정에 이르려면, 그들은 의견차를 끈기있게 좁혀나갈 필요가 있다.

해설_hammer out a difference 의견차를 끈기있게 해결하다

어휘_agreement 합의, 협정, 동의(서) difference 차이 negotiate 협상하다 liberate 해방시키다

정답_(d)

15.

해석_여행 중 병에 걸리지 않기 위해 여행 가기 2주전에 주치의를 만나보라.

해설_'병에 걸리다' 라고 하면 동사와 형용사의 결합 연어로서 fall sick을 사용한다.

어휘_avoid 피하다

정답_(c)

Chapter 2 숙어 (1)

1.

해석_A: Robert는 왜 항상 그렇게 시비조지?

　　　B: 잘은 모르겠지만 그는 항상 다른 사람들에게 불만이 있는 것 같아.

해설_have a bone to pick (with someone) (~에게) 할 말이 있다

어휘_argumentative 논쟁을 좋아하는, 시비를 거는

정답_(a)

2.

해석_A: Jones 씨 부부를 저녁식사에 초대했어. 그들이 술을 마시는지 안마시는지 알고 있니?

　　　B: 그들 둘 다 정말 술을 잘마셔. 준비하는게 좋을 거야.

해설_drink like a fish 술을 물 마시 듯하다, 정말 술을 잘마시다

어휘_be prepared 준비를 하다

정답_(b)

3.

해석_A: 내가 이 비디오를 왜 빌려야 하지?

　　　B: 이 영화 너무 재미있고, 끝나는 순간까지 손에 땀을 쥐게 하거든.

해설_keep someone on the edge of someone's seat 손에 땀을 쥐게 하다

어휘_rent 빌리다

정답_(a)

4.

해석_A: 주식시장이 매우 불안정해. 돈을 좀 넣어놔서 불안하네.

　　　B: 나도 그래. 뭔가 궁지에서 벗어날 만한 방법을 찾아야될 것 같아.

해설_save one's bacon 궁지나 위험 등에서 벗어나다

어휘_unstable 불안정한

정답_(b)

5.

해석_A: 네 가게가 왜 그리 갑작스레 망한 거야?

　　　B: 왜냐면, 내 회계사가 횡령을 해서 난 파산했어.

해설_take someone for a ride ~를 속여서 횡령하다

어휘_bankrupt 파산한

정답_(a)

6.

해석_ A: 디스코 장이 손님들로 빼곡했어.

B: 춤 출 공간이 충분치 않았을 게 분명하겠네.

해설_ be packed in like sardines 빼곡이 들어차다, 만원이다

어휘_ multitude 다수 crowd 군중 throng 다수, 군중

정답_ (d)

7.

해석_ A: 네 라이프 스타일이 왜 그리 갑작스레 바뀐 거야?

B: 지난달에 이 책을 보고 있었는데 그때 내 생각이 완전히 바뀌었어.

해설_ see the light 생각이 갑자기 바뀌다

어휘_ lifestyle 생활 태도

정답_ (c)

8.

해석_ A: 어째서 그들은 바람이 부는 날 그렇게 작은 배를 타고 낚시를 하러 갔지?

B: 예고된 사고였지 뭐.

해설_ (this was) an accident waiting to happen 예고된 사고(였다)

어휘_ windy 바람이 부는 reserve 예약하다

정답_ (b)

9.

해석_ A: Betty, 나는 마음을 고쳐 먹고 매일 일찍 일어날 거야.

B: 내일이 기다려지는데.

해설_ turn over a new leaf 마음을 고쳐 먹다

어휘_ resolution 결심

정답_ (d)

10.

해석_ A: 예전의 계약서를 개작해서 이번 건에도 사용할 수 있지 않을까요?

B: 처음부터 다시 시작해서 완전히 새로운 계약서를 만드는 게 가장 좋겠습니다.

해설_ '아무것도 없는 데서부터' 무엇인가를 만들어 내거나, 어떤 일을 '처음부터 다시' 시작한다고 할 때는 from scratch라는 숙어 표현을 쓴다.

어휘_ adapt 개작하다 injury 상처

정답_ (b)

11.

해석_ A: 어젯밤 미식축구 게임은 어땠어?

B: 최고였어, 우리는 상대 팀을 손쉽게 이겼어.

해설_ wipe the floor with ~를 꺾고 완승하다

어휘_ put on airs 뽐내다

정답_ (d)

12.

해석_ A: 엔진이 역화하는 소리였을 뿐인데, 당신은 왜 도망을 갔나요?

B: 그게 난 총소리인 줄 알고 겁이 났어요.

해설_ get the wind up 겁이 나다

어휘_ backfiring sound 엔진이 역화하는 소리

정답_ (c)

13.

해석_ A: 왜 Simpson네 아버지와 아들은 거의 완전히 대머리지?

B: 누가 알겠어? 집안 내력이겠지.

해설_ run in the family 집안 내력이다

어휘_ bald 대머리의

정답_ (a)

14.

해석_ A: 그는 음정의 차이를 듣지 못해.

B: 그가 음치라는 말이지?

해설_ tone-deaf 음치의

어휘_ musical 음악의 note 음조, 악보 sound-proof 방음의

정답_ (d)

15.

해석_ A: 그 사람 요새 기뻐서 제정신이 아니야. 아내가 아이를 가졌거든.

B: 정말이야? 예정일이 언젠데?

해설_ walk on air 기뻐서 어쩔 줄 모르다

어휘_ expect a baby 임신 중이다 due 예정된

정답_ (b)

Chapter 3 숙어 (2)

1.

해석 A: 그 불은 무시무시했어.

B: 하지만 그건 전화위복이었어. 왜냐하면 이제 사람들은 불에 대해 더 조심할 거거든.

해설 a blessing in disguise 전화위복

어휘 terrifying 무시무시한 disguise 위장 veil 베일, 위장, 변장

정답 (b)

2.

해석 A: 이 오래된 신문들을 모아두어야 할까?

B: 그래, 우리가 창문을 청소할 때 도움이 될지도 몰라.

해설 come in handy 도움이 되다

어휘 save 모으다, 비축하다

정답 (a)

3.

해석 A: 자꾸 말 돌리지 말고, 왜 못하겠는지를 말해봐.

B: 음… 그게 왜냐하면, 난 사실 너랑 있는 게 좀 불편해.

해설 beat about the bush 변죽을 울리다, 돌려 말하다

정답 (a)

4.

해석 A: 자네가 우리의 고객들이 광고에 어떻게 반응하는지 말한 것은 정곡을 찔렀어.

B: 저는 오직 분명해 보이는 것만 말했습니다.

해설 hit the nail on the head 정곡을 찌르다

어휘 respond 반응하다 obvious 명확한

정답 (d)

5.

해석 우리가 실수를 하면, 그는 우리가 그것에 주목하도록 하지만, 그런다고 해서 예전처럼 화를 내지는 않아.

해설 fly off (the handle) 화를 내다

어휘 bring something to our attention 우리가 ~에 주목하게 하다

정답 (c)

6.

해석 A: 이 건물 설계도에 관해서는 우리는 처음으로 되돌아갈 것 같아.

B: 우리가 만들었던 첫 번째 설계도를 감당하지 못한 것은 안된

일이야.

해설 go back to square one 처음으로 되돌아가다

어휘 plan 설계도

정답 (b)

7.

해석 A: 이봐, 그 축하연에 내가 어떤 색의 넥타이를 매고 가야 할 거라 생각해?

B: 사소한 문제를 거창하게 여기지 마. 어느 색이든 괜찮아.

해설 make a mountain out of a molehill 사소한 문제를 거창하게 여기다

어휘 castle 성 fortress 요새

정답 (c)

8.

해석 A: 교장이 퇴임하면, 그의 자리를 대신하는 것은 어려울 거야.

B: 맞아, 그는 이 학교를 위해서 많은 일을 해왔지.

해설 fill someone's shoes 대신하다

어휘 principal 교장 displace 바꾸다, 대체하다

정답 (b)

9.

해석 A: 우리는 Jones 씨를 우리 편으로 만들 필요가 있어.

B: 동의해. 그는 무시 못 할 존재야.

해설 a force to be reckoned with 무시 못 할 존재

어휘 neglect 무시하다

정답 (c)

10.

해석 A: 《카사블랑카》의 여배우 이름이 뭐였더라?

B: 어… 어… 그녀의 이름이 목구멍까지 올라왔는데, 생각이 안 나네.

해설 알고 있는 이름인데 막상 말하려고 하니 '혀끝에서 맴돌기만 하고' 영 생각이 안 나는 경우가 있다. 바로 이럴 때 쓰는 표현이 **on the tip of one's tongue**(목구멍까지 올라왔는데, 입 안에서 뱅뱅 도는데)이다.

정답 (d)

11.

해석 Lizzy는 입에 가득 채우고서는 한입 가득 물과 함께 그것들을 용케 삼켰다.

해설 쉽지 않은 일이지만 그 일을 '해내는 데 성공하다'고 할 때 쓰이는

표현은 **manage to do**이다. 즉, 문맥상 입 안에 가득 찬 음식물(**them**)을 쉽진 않았지만 '용케 삼켰냈으므로(**managed to get them down**)' 빈칸에는 **managed**가 적절하다.

어휘 **get down** 내리다, 삼키다 **confiscate** 징발하다 **drain** 배수하다 **lament** 탄식하다

정답 (a)

12.

해석 원거리 통신은 우리 일상생활에서 현저한 역할을 하고 있으므로 우리 삶에 미치는 원거리 통신의 영향을 이해하기 위해 최선을 다해야 한다.

해설 **play a part**는 '역할을 하다' 란 뜻이어서 **play a (prominent) part in**이라고 하면 '~에서 (현저한) 역할을 하다' 란 의미가 된다.

어휘 **prominent** 현저한 **consequence** 결과 **drain** 배수하다

정답 (c)

13.

해석 당신의 얘기는 말이 안 돼요, **Jack**. 당신의 말은 핵심을 완전히 벗어났어요.

해설 **beside the point** 요점을 벗어나, 핵심을 벗어나, 엉뚱한 (**wide of the mark, beside the mark, irrelevant ↔ to the point**)

어휘 **nonsense** 말도 안 되는 이야기

정답 (c)

14.

해석 그녀가 그 열차를 놓친 것은 참 안된 일이지만, 오늘 아침에 그렇게 늦잠을 잤으니 그래도 싸다.

해설 **it serves someone right (for doing something)** (~했으니) 그러는 것도 당연하다, 그래도 싸다

어휘 **miss** 놓치다 **get up** 일어나다

정답 (c)

15.

해석 만약 당신이 사건을 너무나 강하게 피력한다면 당신의 의견은 분명 평지풍파를 일으킬 것입니다.

해설 **stir the pot**은 반드시 악의적이진 않더라도 고의적으로 성미를 건드리거나 약 올리는 것을 말한다. 또는 언급하고 싶지 않은 사안을 자꾸만 지적하는 것을 뜻하기도 한다.

어휘 **opinion** 의견 **stir** 휘젓다 **lose the day** 패배하다

정답 (d)

Chapter 4 혼동되는 단어

1.

해석 A: **Brown & Cordon** 회사가 어디에 있나요?

B: 이 엘리베이터를 타고 6층에서 내리시면, 접수대가 보입니다.

해설 **exit**은 '탈출하다' 의 의미 외에 '(엘리베이터 등에서) 내리다' 의 의미를 가진다.

어휘 **reception** 접수처, 프런트 **escape** 달아나다

정답 (a)

2.

해석 너는 인사과에 네가 그 직에 적임자라는 것을 알리기 위해서 너의 경력에 대해서 충분히 알려야 한다.

해설 **divulge**는 '누설하다' 의 부정적 의미 외에도 '알리다' 의 긍정적 의미를 지닌 단어이다.

어휘 **convince** 확신시키다 **HR (Human Resources)** 인사 **delude** 속이다 **describe** 묘사하다 **decry** 비난하다

정답 (a)

3.

해석 그들의 은밀한 결혼식은 외떨어진 지역 교회에서 지난 주에 거행되었다.

해설 **alienated**(낯선, 외진) **local church**에서 올린 결혼식에 대해 이야기하고 있으므로 문맥상 '은밀한' 이란 뜻의 **clandestine**이 타당하다.

어휘 **take place** 일어나다, 개최되다 **gorgeous** 화려한 **scandalous** 수치스러운

정답 (b)

4.

해석 그 장교의 군사법원에서의 항소는 증거 불충분으로 기각되었다.

해설 **dismiss**는 일반적인 의미인 '작별하다' 외에 '해고하다' , '기각하다' 의 의미를 가지고 있다.

어휘 **claim** 고소, 요구, 청구 **military court** 군사법원 **insufficient** 불충분한 **evidence** 증거

정답 (d)

5.

해석 그 아이들은 방학 여행에 너무나 들뜬 나머지 떠들썩해져서 흥분을 가라앉혀야만 했다.

해설 인과관계(**so ~ that** 구문)를 통하여 원인을 제대로 파악한다면

그 결과는 쉽게 유추할 수 있고 **and** 다음에 제시된 내용을 보더라
도 **(c)**의 **boisterous**가 답임을 알 수 있다.

어휘_ calm down (흥분 등을) 가라앉히다, 침착하다
lanky 마르고 키 큰 **staid** 안정된, 침착한 **forthright** 솔직한

정답_ (c)

6.

해석_ A: 난 이 물건에 너무 돈을 많이 써서 후회하고 있어요.
　　B: 당신 바가지 쓴 것 같아요.

해설_ 대화의 흐름상 **paying** _________는 '돈을 너무 많이 지불하
다' 는 의미가 되어야 한다. 보기 중 '너무 많이' 란 의미의 부사는
dearly이다. **pay high**도 같은 의미로, 이때는 **highly**가 아니
라 **high**를 쓴다는 점에 주의하도록 한다.

어휘_ rip off 값을 턱없이 요구하다, 도둑질, 사기 **mainly** 주로
sincerely 진정으로

정답_ (b)

7.

해석_ 자신이 갖고 있는 어떤 독단을 없애는 좋은 방법은 자신과는 다른
사회 집단에 속하는 사람들이 갖고 있는 견해에 대해 아는 것이다.

해설_ 빈칸에는 '독단, 독단주의' 를 뜻하는 **dogmatism**이 적절하다.

어휘_ rid yourself of something (좋지 않은 것을) 없애다
positivism 실증, 실증주의 **conservatism** 보수, 보수주의
liberalism 자유주의, 진보주의

정답_ (a)

8.

해석_ K 거리에 비난을 받았던 상점을 설립한 순간부터 **Stanley
Kaplan**은 교육계에서 버림받은 자였다.

해설_ 문맥상 '버림받은 자, 이단아' 를 뜻하는 **pariah**가 적절하다.

어휘_ denounced 비난을 받는 **novice** 풋내기 **ex-convict** 전
과자 **patriot** 애국자

정답_ (a)

9.

해석_ Sally는 산수 문제를 풀 때면 실수를 너무 많이 해서 연필로 쓰는
것만큼이나 자주 지우개를 사용한다.

해설_ 문맥상 '실수', '잘못', '틀림'을 뜻하는 **mistakes**가 적절하다.

어휘_ arithmetic 산수 **as often as** ~만큼 자주

정답_ (b)

10.

해석_ 그 사람들은 최선을 다해서 그 집회를 홍보했다.

해설_ 문장의 흐름상 '홍보했다' 를 뜻하는 **publicized**가 적절하다.

어휘_ laud 칭찬하다 **launch** 착수하다

정답_ (b)

11.

해석_ 의사는 그에게 처방전을 주었는데 다행히 그의 고통은 밤사이 사그
라졌다.

해설_ fortunately(다행히)라는 표현에서 의사의 처방으로 고통이 완화
되었음을 유추할 수 있다. 따라서 '진정되다', '사그라들다' 를 뜻
하는 **subsided**가 적절하다.

어휘_ prescription 처방전 **soar** 치솟다 **appear** 나타나다
expose 드러나다, 노출시키다

정답_ (a)

12.

해석_ 지질학자들은 생명체가 바다 밑바닥에서부터 시작되었을 것이라
는 증거를 제공하는 14억 3천만년 된 심해의 미생물 화석을 발견하
였다.

해설_ originate 발원하다, 시작하다

어휘_ geologist 지질학자 **fossil** 화석 **deep-sea** 깊은 바다의,
심해의 **microbe** 미생물, 세균 **evidence** 증거 **disclose**
폭로하다

정답_ (a)

13.

해석_ 최근 정보는 **FM** 라디오 주파수 그리고 때때로 라디오 프로그램의
파장을 나누면서 컴퓨터의 패킷 단위로 보내진다.

해설_ packet 묶음

어휘_ frequency 주파수 **wavelength** 파장 **class** 종류, 부류
bundle 다발

정답_ (a)

14.

해석_ 대서양 연안의 아프리카 국가들은 잠정적 연간 어획량의 절반 이상
을 강탈해가는 불법 어로를 감시하기 위하여 위성 감시를 사용할
것이다.

해설_ which 뒤의 **robs**를 참조. 자신들로부터 **rob**, 즉 '강탈' 해가는
것을 방지하고자 하는 것이므로 단순히 '포획' 을 뜻하는
catching보다는 불법성을 띠는 '밀렵', '밀어' 를 뜻하는
poaching이 적절하다.

어휘_ Atlantic 대서양 **coastline** 해안선 **satellite** 인공위성
surveillance 감시, 망보기 **rob** 강탈하다, 빼앗다
potential 가능한, 잠재하는 **annual** 1년의, 해마다의

정답_ (c)

15.

해석_ 폭풍우로 인해 발사 준비에 계속 지장이 있었지만, 토요일에는 날씨가 좋아질 가능성이 80%였다.

해설_ but 앞의 문장을 직역하면 '폭풍우가 발사 준비를 계속 방해했다' 이므로 빈칸에는 '방해했다'는 뜻의 동사 **plagued**가 적절하다.

어휘_ **launch** (어뢰 · 유도탄 · 로켓 등을) 발사 **preparation** 준비 **chance** 가능성, 기회 **assist** 거들다, 원조하다

정답_ (c)

Chapter 5 2어동사

1.

해석_ 평결은 다양한 전문가 집단이 어떤 동기로 얼마나 충실하고도 유능하게 증언을 하느냐에 따라 달라질 수 있다.

해설_ **hinge on** ~의 여하에 달려 있다

어휘_ **verdict** (배심원이 재판장에게 제출하는) 평결 **motive** 동기, 목적 **loyalty** 충성, 성실 **competence** 적격, 능력 **slate** 후보자 **expert** 전문가 **witness** 증인 **divergent** (의견 등이) 다른 **opinion** 의견, 견해

정답_ (c)

2.

해석_ **A:** 난 이제 갈래. 더 오래 있을 거야?

　　B: 응, 퇴근하기 전에 일을 마무리하고 싶어. 내일 봐.

해설_ **wrap things up** 마무리하다

어휘_ **quit for the day** 하루를 끝내다, 하루를 마무리 짓다

정답_ (a)

3.

해석_ **A:** 이번 주의 스키 여행은 1인당 450달러가 들어.

　　B: 와! 나는 빼줘. 나는 그렇게 돈이 많지 않아.

해설_ **count someone out** ~를 빼다

어휘_ **per** ~마다 **include** 포함하다 **regard** 여기다, 간주하다

정답_ (a)

4.

해석_ 결과적으로 석유회사들이 미 정부로부터 소득세를 어림잡아 30억 달러를 탕감받는데도 소비자들은 연료비를 더 많이 낸다.

해설_ **write off** (장부에서) 없애 주다, (빚을) 덜어 주다, 탕감 받다(**take off the books**), 감가상각하다(**reduce the value of**)

어휘_ **result** 결과 **consumer** 소비자 **estimated** 견적의, 추측의 **income tax** 소득세

정답_ (b)

5.

해석_ 여당의 반대에도 불구하고, 세금 문제에 대해서 정부는 조금도 물러서지 않고 있다.

해설_ **back down** 물러나다

어휘_ **boil down** 압축되다, 요약되다 **bring down** 사임하게 하다

정답_ (a)

6.

해석_ A: 이런, 중간고사까지는 고작 3일 남았는데, 아무것도 기억이
　　　 안 나.
　　 B: 걱정하지 마. 내가 너의 기억을 되살리는 것을 도와줄게.

해설_ brush up ~의 공부를 다시 시작하다, ~의 기억을 새로이 하다

어휘_ midterm (학기 · 임기 등의)중간(기) memory 기억
　　 revise 정정하다

정답_ (a)

7.

해석_ A: 도대체 상사한테 왜 말대꾸를 한 거야?
　　 B: 왜냐하면 동료들이 주변에서 날 부추겼거든.

해설_ egg someone on은 누군가에게 뭔가를 하도록 부추기는 것
　　 을 뜻한다.

어휘_ talk back 말대꾸하다 colleague 동료

정답_ (c)

8.

해석_ A: 팔은 왜 부러진 거야?
　　 B: 어제 자전거를 타다가 넘어졌어.

해설_ be knocked off 넘어지다

어휘_ be keeled over 전복되다 fall apart 흐트러지다

정답_ (a)

9.

해석_ 약탈은 도시 곳곳에서 돌발적으로 일어났고, 몇몇 외국 대사관들은
　　 비필수 요원들과 부양 가족들을 소개시켰다.

해설_ break out 돌발하다(burst out)

어휘_ loot 약탈하다 scattered 산재된 embassy 대사관
　　 evacuate 비우다, 피난시키다 dependent 부양가족
　　 abide by (약속을)지키다 bring up 양육하다(raise,
　　 educate, nurse) result in ~ 결과를 이끌어내다

정답_ (b)

10.

해석_ 우리는 Motor Cara Model EC-331을 구매하고 싶은데, 귀
　　 사에 주문하게 되어 기쁩니다.

해설_ be in the market for ~을 구매하려고 하다(be seeking
　　 to buy, want to buy)

어휘_ place an order 주문하다
　　 be up to one's ears[neck] in ~으로 정신이 없다, 바쁘다

정답_ (a)

11.

해석_ 국제연합의 목적은, 헌장에서 천명한 대로, 세계의 평화와 안보를
　　 유지하는 것이다.

해설_ lay down 선언하다, 천명하다, 규정하다(declare officially,
　　 prescribe)

어휘_ purpose 목적 United Nations 국제연합, 유엔 Charter
　　 헌장 maintain 유지하다 security 안보 dawn on 이해
　　 되기 시작하다 gain on 접근하다, 추격하다 work out 성취
　　 하다, 가져오다

정답_ (b)

12.

해석_ 처음 이 반을 맡았을 때 자신감과 목적성이 없는 학생들이 너무 많
　　 아서 난 이 학생들을 바로 세우기 위해 노력하고 있다.

해설_ straighten out 똑바르게 하다, ~을 명료하게 하다, 정리하다

어휘_ lack 부족 confidence 자신감 motivation 동기
　　 suit up 제복을 입히다 take over 인계받다, 양도받다

정답_ (c)

13.

해석_ 나는 과거에 자신감이 넘치는 편이었다. 하지만 최근에 내 여자친
　　 구가 날 버리고 떠났다. 그 이후로 나는 자신감을 모두 잃어버렸기
　　 때문에 정말이지 그녀는 나를 무력하게 만들어버렸다.

해설_ psych out 무력하게 만들다

어휘_ overconfident 자부심이 강한 take someone out ~을
　　 기분 전환시키다, ~에게 근심을 잊게 하다 burn oneself out
　　 시력을 다하다, 과로로 일찍 죽다

정답_ (a)

14.

해석_ 전 재산을 모두 쏟아 붓는 것이기 때문에 사업의 조사를 더 깊게 하
　　 는 것은 좋은 생각이다.

해설_ look into ~을 조사하다, 수사하다(see into, investigate)

어휘_ take hold of ~을 붙잡다 get through ~을 겪다, ~을 통과
　　 하다

정답_ (d)

15.

해석_ 그가 너무 빨리 말해서 그가 무엇을 말하는지 기록하는 데에 어려
　　 웠다.

해설_ take down 적다, 기록하다(write down, jut down, put
　　 down, record)

어휘_ put forward 제안하다 follow up 추적하다 hand in 제
출하다

정답_ (b)

Chapter 6 표현

1.

해석_ A: 뮤지컬 《5번가에서》는 회전 장치 무대로 유명하지.

B: 회전 장치 무대? 아, 그래 이제 생각났어.

해설_ **ring a bell**은 공감을 불러일으키거나 무언가를 생각나게 한다는
뜻이다. 반면 **play by ear**은 악보 없이 연주하다, **be booked
up**은 선약이 있다, 그리고 **be tied up**은 단단히 묶이다 또는 결
혼했다는 뜻이므로 대화의 흐름상 **Oh, yes**. 다음에는 **It rings a
bell**.이 가장 자연스럽다.

어휘_ **revolving** 회전하는

정답_ (d)

2.

해석_ A: 대학에서 날 받아주게 될 것인지에 대한 소식을 기다리자니 미
치겠어.

B: 곧 알게 될 테니 너무 초조해 말라고!

해설_ **Hang in there!** 너무 초조해 마, 참고 기다려!

어휘_ **go nuts** 미칠 지경이다

정답_ (b)

3.

해석_ A: 너 진담인 건 아니겠지? 그녀는 아기처럼 행동한다고.

B: 농담 아니야. 그녀는 결혼하려고 별짓을 다한다고.

해설_ **I kid you not.** 혹은 **I am not kidding. / I am not
joking.** 등은 '농담이 아니에요.' 란 의미이다.

어휘_ **serious** 진지한, 진담의 **get married** 결혼하다

정답_ (a)

4.

해석_ A: 사장이 내 고용 계약을 연장해 줄까?

B: 꿈꾸지 마. 잘 나갈 때 그만두는 게 좋아.

해설_ **Forget it.**은 **Drop the subject.**라는 의미로 쓰인다. 따라서
더 이상 말하지 말라, 즉 관두어라, 꿈도 꾸지 말라는 뜻이다.

어휘_ **extend** 연장하다

정답_ (a)

5.

해석_ A: 나는 **Burton** 교수님이 정말 무서워.

B: 그에 대해 걱정하지 마. 그는 말은 거칠지만 본성은 그렇게 나
쁘지 않아.

해설_ **One's bark is worse than one's bite.** 말은 거칠지만 본

성은 그렇게 나쁘지 않다.

어휘_ gnaw (앞니로) 갉다, 물어뜯다 bullet 총탄 shot 발포, 발사

정답_ (c)

6.

해석_ **A:** 그 스웨터 누구 것이야?

　　B: 나도 몰라. 나는 그것을 본 적이 없어.

해설_ **You got me (there).**는 '모르겠다'를 뜻한다. 하지만 문맥에 따라선 **I get you.** 즉 **I understand you.**(무슨 말인지 이해합니다.)가 되기도 한다.

정답_ (b)

7.

해석_ **A: Jane!** 너를 여기에서 만나게 되다니!

　　B: Kathy, 네가 이곳에 올 거라고 나도 생각 못했어!

해설_ **Fancy meeting you here!** 너를 여기에서 만나게 되다니!

정답_ (c)

8.

해석_ **A:** 네가 봉급을 올려 받을 만한 자격이 있다고 사장에게 그냥 말해버려.

　　B: 알아, 하지만 말이 쉽지.

해설_ **Easier said than done.** 말이 쉽지. (행동하는 건 어려워.)

어휘_ **deserve** ~할 만한 자격이 있다 **raise** 봉급 인상(**pay raise**)

정답_ (c)

9.

해석_ **A: Bob,** 너 일 년에 얼마나 버니?

　　B: 내 일이야. 네가 상관할 바가 아니라고!

해설_ **Mind your own business!** 네가 상관할 바가 아니야!

어휘_ **That's for me to know.** 내가 알아서 할 일이다, 나의 일이다, 네가 알 바 아니다.

정답_ (c)

10.

해석_ **A:** 소비자들은 형편없는 품질의 제품에 질렸어.

　　B: 제조업체들은 그들의 제품 기준을 올릴 필요가 있어.

해설_ **be fed up with** ~에 질리다, 신물이 나다

어휘_ **consumer** 소비자 **poor quality** 품질이 나쁜 **product** 상품 **manufacturer** 제조자 **raise** 올리다 **standard** 기준

정답_ (c)

11.

해석_ **A:** 이 체리 파이 정말 맛있다!

　　B: 작은 조각이 하나 남았어. 네가 먹도록 해.

해설_ **Be my guest.** ① 먼저 하세요. ② 좋을 대로 하세요. (상대의 간단한 부탁에 예, 그러세요**;** 좋으실 대로 하세요)

정답_ (a)

12.

해석_ **A:** 나는 그들이 현명하게 그렇게 빨리 결혼한 것이었으면 좋겠어.

　　B: 오직 시간만이 말해주겠지.

해설_ **(Only) Time will tell.** (오직) 시간이 말해주겠지.

정답_ (b)

13.

해석_ **A:** 이 판매 보고서는 훌륭해 보이지만 내용은 별로야.

　　B: 맞아. 콩 심은 데 콩 나고 팥 심은 데 팥 나는 법이야.

해설_ **Garbage in, garbage out.** 콩 심은 데 콩 나고 팥 심은 데 팥 난다.

정답_ (b)

14.

해석_ **A: Marsha**가 치통으로 오늘 일할 수 없다고 전화가 왔어요.

　　B: 더 이상 못 참겠어! 그녀에게 전화해서 해고됐다고 말해주세요.

해설_ **That's the last straw!** 더 이상 못 참겠어!

어휘_ **call in** 전화로 보고하다 **toothache** 치통 **patience** 인내

정답_ (c)

15.

해석_ **A:** 우리는 절대 사진 콘테스트에서 우승 못 할 거야.

　　B: 낙담하지 마. 계속 노력해보자.

해설_ **Never say die.** 낙담하지 마.

정답_ (a)

Chapter 7 내용 혼동어

1.

해석_ A: 우리가 목표했던 모금액에 도달했나?

B: 사실, 익명의 기부자가 우리의 목적을 달성하는 데 도움을 줬어.

해설_ score는 점수에 도달했을 때 쓰는 표현이다.

어휘_ fund raising 모금 anonymous 익명의

정답_ (a)

2.

해석_ 일본 정부는 1990년대 말 이후 저출산율 때문에 우려하고 있다.

해설_ 문맥상 low birth _________가 '저출산율' 이란 의미가 될 수 있도록 빈칸에는 '비율' 이란 뜻의 단어가 적절하다. (b)의 ratio 는 양자 비교 시의 비율을 뜻하고, (d)의 proportion은 전에 대비한 비율을 나타낸다. 따라서 특정 기간 내의 특정 횟수를 뜻하는 일반적인 의미의 '비율' 을 뜻하는 (a)의 rate이 정답이다.

정답_ (a)

3.

해석_ 군사 법정의 배심원은 그의 관련성에 의구심이 던져지는 증언에도 불구하고 한 군인에게 14세의 이라크 소녀와 그녀의 가족을 강간하고 죽인 죄를 인정했다.

해설_ 사건이나 일에의 관련성을 나타낼 때 involvement를 쓴다. chemistry는 관계의 의미 중에서도 사람 사이에 죽이 맞는지 여부를 나타낼 때 쓴다. relation은 위치나 지위 등의 상호 관계에서 사용한다.

어휘_ jury 배심원 rape 강간 murder 살인 testimony 증언

정답_ (b)

4.

해석_ 환경 운동 단체는 강가에 새로운 공장이 생기는 것을 막는 것에 대하여 지지를 이끌어내기 위해서 대중 집회를 소집했다.

해설_ 같은 금지의 의미라도 법적으로 금지하는 것을 ban이라고 하고, embargo는 통상 금지, 항해 금지를 의미한다. taboo는 관습상, 전통상의 금지를 의미한다.

어휘_ construct 건설하다 provocation 선동

정답_ (a)

5.

해석_ 조종사의 보고에 의하면 폭풍 때문에 시야가 제로가 되었다고 한다.

해설_ zero visibility는 기상 용어로 '시정이 0' 이어서 아무것도 안 보인다는 뜻이다. sight는 within sight(보이는 거리에 있는), out

어휘_ range 범위 limit 한계

정답_ (a)

6.

해석_ A: 머리스타일이 바뀌어서, 사장님 사모님을 못 알아봤어.

B: 나도 그래. 그녀가 이 말을 들으면 칭찬으로 생각할 걸.

해설_ 사람이나 사물을 '인지하다, 알아보다' 라고 할 때는 recognize 를, 어떤 사실을 '깨달아서 다시금 알게 되다' 고 할 때는 realize 를 쓴다.

어휘_ Join the club. 이쪽도 마찬가지다. take something as a compliment 칭찬으로 받아들이다 notice 알아채다

정답_ (c)

7.

해석_ A: 저는 Barker 씨를 만나고 싶어요.

B: 약속은 하셨나요?

해설_ 사람 사이에 미리 정해진 공식적인 약속은 appointment를 사용한다.

정답_ (a)

8.

해석_ A: Packson 선생님 진료를 받고 싶은데요.

B: 언제가 가능한지 봐드릴게요. 내일 오후 3시 어떠세요?

해설_ available은 free와 마찬가지로 어떤 사람이 무엇인가를 할 '시간이 있는' 이란 의미로 쓰여, 상대방에게 '지금 시간 있냐?(Are you available now?)' 고 물을 때나 이 대화에서와 같이 누가 언제 시간이 되는지 봐줄게(Let me see when he is available.)와 같은 식으로 자주 쓰인다.

어휘_ see a doctor 병원에 가다, 진료 받으러 가다 accessible 접근하기 쉬운, 면회하기 쉬운 liable 책임 있는

정답_ (b)

9.

해석_ A: 우리가 점심으로 근사한 스테이크를 먹으면 오후에 일을 더 잘 할 거라 생각해.

B: 그게 말야, 나랑 생각이 똑같구나.

해설_ Great minds think alike. 나랑 생각이 똑같구나.

어휘_ ponder 숙고하다 recall 생각해내다 reflect 반영하다

정답_ (a)

10.

해석 A: 왜 Albert는 오늘 모든 사람들에게 불평이지?

B: 그 친구는 요즘 좀 우울하거든. 그래서 동병상련으로 다른 사람의 흠을 잡는 거지.

해설 Misery loves company. ① 동병상련이다. ② 유유상종이다.

어휘 critical 비판적인, 흠을 잘 잡는

정답 (b)

11.

해석 A: 영업부는 30세 미만의 잠재적 고객에 초점을 맞추기로 했어.

B: 여자와 남자 모두 포함하는 거야?

해설 zero in on something 조준을 (목표에) 맞추다; ~에 포화를 집중하다

어휘 sales department 영업부 prospective 예상된, 기대되는 target 목표, 과녁

정답 (c)

12.

해석 심지어 과학자들에게조차도, 암석과 광물의 차이를 구별하는 것은 미묘하고 어려운 일이다.

해설 (a)는 의미는 통하지만, the difference와 어울리지 않는다.

어휘 rock 암석 mineral 광물 discriminate 차별하다
hammer out (금속 따위)를 두드려 펴서 모양을 만들다
iron out 다림질하다, 주름을 펴다

정답 (b)

13.

해석 TV에서 수재민들의 참상이 보도되는 것을 보고 마음이 동한 국민들은 음식, 담요, 옷 등을 기부했다.

해설 flood victim(수재민)이므로 곤경을 뜻하는 predicament가 적절하다.

어휘 moved by ~에 의해 영향을 받은, 감격한 flood 홍수
blanket 담요 plague 흑사병 doom 운명 dearth 기근

정답 (d)

14.

해석 로봇을 이용해 흙과 얼음을 파는 기계가 화성을 향해 토요일 발사되었다. NASA가 기대하고 있는 4억 2천 2백만 마일의 여정에 오른 이 로봇은 내년 봄에 정점에 올라 최초로 적색 별(화성)의 극지방에 착륙하게 될 것이다.

해설 어떤 일이 '정점에 올라 ~하게 되다' 고 할 때는 culminate in을 쓴다. 또한 A culminate in B는 'A로 인해 B라는 결과를 초래하다' 라는 의미로도 쓰인다는 것을 알아두자.

어휘 robotic 로봇을 이용하는, 로봇식의 digger 굴착기
landing 착륙 Arctic Circle 북극권

정답 (a)

15.

해석 내 룸메이트는 공과금을 분담하자는 제안에 동의했지만, 아직 자기 몫을 내지 않았다.

해설 서로 협의에 의해서 할당을 한 몫에 대해서는 share를 쓴다.

어휘 accept 받아들이다 proposal 제안 divide 나누다
utility bill 공과금 lot 추첨 sort 종류 quota 할당량

정답 (a)

Chapter 8 형태 혼동어

1.

해석_ A: 어떻게 **Edison**이 그 당시로는 거액인 4만 달러를 벌었지?
B: 주식 시세 표시기를 개량했어.
해설_ a considerable sum 상당한 액수, 거액
어휘_ eventually 결국, 마침내 earn 얻게 하다 improvement 개선
정답_ (a)

2.

해석_ **John**은 구직광고를 찾기 위하여 신문을 자세히 찾아보려고 한다.
해설_ canvass는 '선거운동하다' 또는 '샅샅이 뒤지다' 의 의미를 가진다. 그러나 canvas는 화폭으로 쓰이는 강한 천을 의미한다.
어휘_ converse 변환하다 compass 에워싸다
정답_ (a)

3.

해석_ **Paul Bunyan**과 **Pecos Bill**의 전설적인 업적은 상상이 빚어낸 것이다. 반면, **Washington**과 **Lincoln**에 관한 소위 전설은 대부분 그 두 대통령이 가지고 있던 실제 자질들을 과장한 것이다.
해설_ imaginary 상상의
어휘_ legend 전설 exaggeration 과장
정답_ (b)

4.

해석_ 일본인들은 환율이 자신들에게 유리할 때는 종종 국경을 넘나드는 여행을 했다.
해설_ cross-boarder 국경을 넘는 cross-country 전국의, 국토를 횡단하여 cross-examining 반대 심문하는 cross-over 교차로
어휘_ exchange rate 환율 preferable 나은, 유리한
정답_ (a)

5.

해석_ 정부 관리는 거대 합병 계약에서 불법적인 공모가 있었는지를 의심했다.
해설_ collusion은 '공모' 의 의미, collision은 '충돌' 의 의미를 가진다.
어휘_ suspect 의심하다 merger 합병
정답_ (a)

6.

해석_ A: 집으로 운전해서 돌아오는데 계속 내 뒤를 따라오던 빨간 차가 보이더니 갑자기 사라져버렸지.
B: 내가 볼 땐 아무도 널 미행하지 않았어. 그저 네가 지나치게 의식하는 것뿐이야.
해설_ 어떤 일에 '병적으로 집착하거나 의식하는', 즉 '편집증적인' 성향을 영어로 paranoid라고 한다.
어휘_ parallel 평행하는 paranormal 과학적으로 알 수가 없는 paralyzed 마비된
정답_ (d)

7.

해석_ A: 오늘 수학 시험은 식은 죽 먹기였어요.
B: 너무 그렇게 자신만만해 하지 말거라.
해설_ overconfident 지나치게 자신만만한
어휘_ breeze 용이한 일, 산들바람 overburdened 과로한, 지나치게 부담을 지운 overrated 과대평가된 overdone 너무 익힌, 과로한, 과장된
정답_ (a)

8.

해석_ 우체국들은 **Meimpsrial Day**를 준수하여 다음 주 월요일에는 문을 닫는다.
해설_ 문맥상 in_____of는 '~날을 준수하여' 라는 의미가 되어야 한다. 따라서 빈칸에는 '준수' 를 뜻하는 observance가 적절하다. 〈in observance of + 국경일〉의 형태로 묶어서 익혀두는 것이 좋다. (a)의 observation은 '관찰' 을 뜻하므로 혼동하지 않도록 한다.
어휘_ Memorial Day 미국의 현충일(대다수의 주에서 5월의 마지막 월요일)
정답_ (d)

9.

해석_ **Tim**은 자신이 수집한 우표의 가치가 오르기를 바랐지만, 가치가 없어져버리고 말았다.
해설_ appreciate 가치가 상승하다
어휘_ worthless 가치 없는 perish 소멸하다 subside 가라앉다 depreciate 가치가 저하되다
정답_ (c)

10.

해석_ 연설 중에 대통령은 환경 문제들에 대해 전 세계가 같이 고려해야

한다고 몇 번이나 역설했다.

해설 __________ **the need for a global approach to environmental problems**를 직역하면 '환경 문제에 대해 전 세계적인 접근의 필요성을 ~했다' 가 된다. 즉 '세계가 다함께 나서 환경 문제를 해결할 수 있도록 해야 한다는 것을 ~했다' 는 의미이다. 따라서 빈칸에는 '역설했다, 강조했다' 는 뜻의 **underscored**가 어울린다. **underscore the need for**(~에 대한 필요성을 역설하다)로 통째 외워두면 유리하다.

어휘 **environmental problem** 환경 문제 **undergo** 겪다 **undermine** ~의 밑을 파다 **undertake** 맡다

정답 (a)

11.

해석 과학 그 자체는 도덕적으로 중립이다. 다시 말해 과학 수단은 그것이 사용되는 목적의 가치에는 무관심하다.

해설 **that is**(다시 말해, 즉) 이하에는 바로 앞에서 언급한 말을 부연 설명하는 내용이 나와야 한다. 따라서 앞서 언급한 '과학이 도덕적으로 중립' 이라는 말과 같은 선상의 의미가 될 수 있도록 빈칸에는 '무관심한' 이란 의미의 **indifferent**가 적절하다.

어휘 **morally** 도덕적으로 **neutral** 중립적인 **end** 목적, 결과 **means** 수단 **be used for** ~에 사용되다

정답 (b)

12.

해석 우리 부모님은 긴 예배 시간 내내 여동생이 그들 사이에 앉아 교회 의자에서 몸을 뒤척이는 게 신경이 쓰이셨지만, 그래도 여동생이 예배 중에 정중하게 행동하도록 가르치기로 결심하셨다.

해설 문맥상 **behave_____**는 '정중하게 행동하다' 는 의미가 되어야 한다. 보기 중 (a) **respectively**는 '각각' 이란 의미이고, (b) **respectably**는 '존경할 만하여' 란 의미이며, (d)는 아예 영어에 있지도 않은 어휘이다. (c) **respectfully**가 '정중하게, 공손히' 란 의미로 빈칸에 적절하다.

어휘 **be determined to do** ~하기로 결정하다 **behave** 행동하다 **in church** 예배 중에 **service** 예배 **squirm** (좁은 공간에서) 몸을 뒤척이다 **pew** (나무로 만든 긴) 교회 의자

정답 (c)

13.

해석 Betty의 엄마는 Betty가 운동하다 다치자 그 지역 최고의 정형 외과 의사에게 보냈다.

해설 **orthopedist** 정형 외과 의사

어휘 **orthodontist** 치열 교정 의사 **optician** 안경상(商)

oculist 안과 의사

정답 (a)

14.

해석 사람들이 대규모로 대도시에서 시골로 가는 것은 8월 첫째 주에 정점에 달한다.

해설 **exodus** 대규모 이동

어휘 **reach a peak** 정점에 달하다 **exertion** 노력 **extinction** 멸종 **excess** 초과

정답 (b)

15.

해석 의사의 명령에 반하여, 그 여성은 계속 야근을 해서 건강에 해를 입었다.

해설 **detriment** 상해

어휘 **depreciation** 가치 하락 **demolition** 파괴 **derision** 비웃음

정답 (c)

Chapter 9 다의어

1.

해석_ A: 하와이에서 1주일간의 공짜 호텔방? 조건이 뭐죠?

　　　B: 하와이까지의 비행기 티켓은 정규 가격에 사셔야 해요.

해설_ What's the catch? 조건이 무엇입니까? 여기서의 **catch**는 '잡다' 의 의미가 아니라 '조건' 의 의미로 쓰인 것이다.

어휘_ regular price 정규 가격, 정가

정답_ (a)

2.

해석_ A: 이 프로그램을 정말로 성공시킨 사람은 바로 우리야.

　　　B: 공적이 있는 사람에게 공을 돌려야지. **Tom**의 도움도 필수적이었어.

해설_ Give credit where credit is due. 공적이 있는 사람에게 공을 돌리다. 이때 **credit**은 '공로' 를 뜻한다.

어휘_ indispensable 필수적인

정답_ (c)

3.

해석_ 마라톤에 참가하면 기분이 좋아질 뿐만 아니라 좋은 일을 하게 되는 것이다.

해설_ good cause 대의

어휘_ participate in ~에 참가하다

정답_ (b)

4.

해석_ 너는 결코 젖은 손으로 전기 기구를 만지면 안 된다.

해설_ account가 여기에서는 다른 의미보다는 조건이라는 의미로 보아야 한다. 즉 '어떤 조건에서도 결코' 를 **on no account** 라고 한다.

어휘_ appliance 가전기구

정답_ (a)

5.

해석_ 공장에서의 힘든 일로부터의 스트레스와 피로가 직원들을 지치게 만든다.

해설_ wear는 여기서 '(옷을) 입다' 의 뜻이 아니라 '피로하게 만들다' 의 의미를 가진다.

어휘_ fatigue 피로　**gear** 매진하다, 애쓰다

정답_ (b)

6.

해석_ A: 누가 네 형인 **Sam**이니?

　　　B: 동상 근처에서 서성이는 사람이야.

해설_ linger 서성이다, 우물쭈물하다

어휘_ rally 결집하다　**derange** 흐트러뜨리다　**suffocate** 질식시키다

정답_ (a)

7.

해석_ A: Paul, 자전거 차선이 없는 데서 자전거를 타면 위험해.

　　　B: 알아요. 그러나 난 항상 조심해요.

해설_ lane 차선, 차로

정답_ (a)

8.

해석_ A: Jane이 학교에 가고 싶지 않다고 그래.

　　　B: 어째서? 학교 불량배들이 걔를 괴롭히니?

해설_ bully는 불량배들이 '괴롭히다' 의 뜻이다.

어휘_ tolerate 너그럽게 대하다　**ban** 금지하다

정답_ (a)

9.

해석_ A: 나 피곤해. 식사 좀 차려 줄래?

　　　B: 나도야. 피자를 배달시키는 게 어때?

해설_ fix the table 식사를 차리다, 준비하다

어휘_ arrange 정돈하다

정답_ (a)

10.

해석_ A: 우리 아들은 공부는 안 하고 밤새도록 친구들과 싸돌아 다녀요.

　　　B: 걱정하지 마세요. 그런 건 십대들이 보통 겪게 되는 과정일 거에요.

해설_ 문맥상 ______ **which teens usually experience**는 '십대들이 보통 거치는[겪는] 과정' 이란 의미가 되어야 한다. 따라서 빈칸에는 '과정' 이란 의미의 **phase**가 적절하다. **phenomena**는 '현상' 을 뜻하는 **phenomenon**의 복수형으로 문맥상 적절치 못하다.

어휘_ hang out with ~와 싸돌아 다니며 놀다　**scala** (물리학 용어) '벡터(vector)' 가 방향과 크기를 동시에 나타내는 개념이라면 '스케일러' 는 크기만을 나타내는 개념을 말함

정답_ (a)

11.

해석_ 은행에서 그런 식으로 돈을 빌리면 최소한 갚아야 하는 돈이 너무
많아.

해설_ **minimal** 최소한

정답_ (a)

12.

해석_ 대부분의 대기업들의 예에서 알 수 있는 것처럼 성공하려면 효과적
인 의사소통이 극히 중요하다.

해설_ **critical** 결정적인, 중대한

어휘_ **effective** 효과적인 **communication** 의사소통

정답_ (a)

13.

해석_ 세계의 일부 지역에서는 매일 사냥한 동물을 먹는다.

해설_ **wild game**에서의 **game**은 '게임' 이 아니라 '사냥감' 의 의미
로서 쓰인 것이다. **clam**(조개)은 사냥을 통해서 잡는 것은 아니다.

정답_ (a)

14.

해석_ 더 많은 정보가 대중에게 이용 가능해지자 새로운 댐에 대한 반대
는 추진력을 얻었다.

해설_ **momentum**은 원래 '운동량, 힘' 의 의미이지만, 여기에서는
'추진력, 동력' 의 의미로 쓰였다.

어휘_ **moderation** 절제, 완화 **monopoly** 독점 **mobility** 이동성

정답_ (d)

15.

해석_ 여당은 선거에서 압승을 거두었다. 사람들이 대부분 여당을 지
지했다.

해설_ **landslide** (선거 등에서) 압승

어휘_ **ruling party** 여당 **avalanche** 눈사태, 산사태
seismology 지진학

정답_ (a)

Final Test (1)

1.

해석_ A: 우리 아버지는 나의 선택에 대해서 절대 반대 하셨어.

　　　B: 그러면, 어떻게 설득을 했었니?

해설_ **be dead set against** 절대 반대하다

어휘_ **persuade** 설득하다 **opinion** 의견 **intention** 의도

정답_ (c)

2.

해석_ A: 오늘 저녁식사에 초대하고 싶군요.

　　　B: 다음 기회로 미룰 수 있을까요?

해설_ **rain check** (지금은 사양하지만 나중에 요구함) 후일의 약속, 초
대의 연기

어휘_ **invite** 초대하다

정답_ (c)

3.

해석_ A: 무슨 일이야? 바지가 온통 진흙투성이네.

　　　B: 오렌지 껍질에 넘어졌어.

해설_ **be plastered with** ~투성이다

어휘_ **trousers** 바지

정답_ (b)

4.

해석_ A: 저 너무 실망했어요. 더 잘 할 수 있었을 텐데요.

　　　B: 그런데 전 이해를 못하겠어요. (어떤 부분이 맘에 안 드시는
지) 지적해 주시겠어요?

해설_ **point out** 지적하다

어휘_ **explain** 설명하다

정답_ (d)

5.

해석_ A: 결정을 내리기가 힘들군.

　　　B: 결정을 해! 계속 잘 하던가, 아님 그만두던가.

해설_ **Shape up or ship out**. 열심히 하지 않을 사람은 나가라.

어휘_ **make up one's mind** 마음을 정하다, 결정을 내리다

정답_ (d)

6.

해석_ A: 난 거의 밖에서 먹지 않아.

　　　B: 나도 마찬가지야, 나도 거의 외식은 안 해.

해설_ once in a blue moon 아주 드물게
어휘_ piece of cake 쉬운 일 habitual 습관적인
정답_ (b)

7.

해석_ A: 역사는 과거의 단순한 연대기적 기록 이상이어야 한다고 난 생
　　 각해.
　　 B: 맞아. 사건을 해석하고 정리하는 데 있어서 약간의 주관적 가치
　　　 판단은 불가피하지.
해설_ subjective judgement 주관적 가치 판단
어휘_ annalistic 연대기적 inevitable 불가피한 order 배열하
　　 다, 정리하다 interpretation 해석 decadent 쇠퇴기에 접어
　　 든, 퇴폐적인
정답_ (c)

8.

해석_ A: 그 앤 의지할 수 있는 생계수단이 없어.
　　 B: 왜 그 앤 일 안 해?
해설_ depend 의지하다
어휘_ means 수단
정답_ (b)

9.

해석_ A: 네 핸드폰을 빌릴 수 있겠니? 내 것은 배터리가 닳았어.
　　 B: 물론, 이거 써.
해설_ 배터리가 다 닳은 상태를 flat이라고도 한다.
어휘_ Help yourself. 그렇게 하세요, 좋을대로 하세요. vacant 빈
　　 fiery 불같은
정답_ (b)

10.

해석_ A: Tom은 휴가 기간에 파리에서 호텔에 아파 누워 지냈어.
　　 B: 인생이란 그런 거지, 그 사람 꽤 실망했겠는 걸.
해설_ That's the way the ball bounces.는 "인생이란 그런 거
　　 지."란 뜻의 관용 표현이므로 표현을 통째 익혀두어야 풀 수 있는 문
　　 제이다. 같은 의미로 That's the way cookie crumbles.
　　 라고도 한다.
어휘_ sick in bed 아파서 드러누운 must have been 분명 ~였
　　 을 것이다 hop 깡충깡충 뛰다
정답_ (a)

11.

해석_ A: 이미 벌어진 일이야.
　　 B: 알아. 하지만 정말이지 걱정을 떨쳐버릴 수가 없는 걸.
해설_ put something to rest 사라지게 하다, 잠재우다, 떨쳐버리다
어휘_ simply 다만, 정말로
정답_ (d)

12.

해석_ A: Bob은 그 사고를 보고 어떻게 했어?
　　 B: 걔, 정말 침착했어. 부상자들을 돕고 경찰을 불렀어.
해설_ cool, calm and collected 정말 침착한
어휘_ serene (바다 등이) 고요한 tranquil (장소, 환경이) 조용한
정답_ (c)

13.

해석_ A: 이렇게 늦은 시간에 방문하는 건 너무 실례가 아닐까?
　　 B: 이 시간이 너무 늦었다고 생각해? 아침까지 기다려야 하나?
해설_ unholy hour 늦은 시간 late 늦은
어휘_ postpone 연기하다
정답_ (a)

14.

해석_ A: Larry가 직장을 잃었다고 일전에 Jane이 말했어.
　　 B: 그가 기대에 부응하지 못했기 때문에, 그들이 그를 해고한 거야.
해설_ cut the mustard 기대에 부응하다, 기준[목표]에 달하다
어휘_ fire 해고하다
정답_ (d)

15.

해석_ A: 평화와 발전은 우리가 생각하는 것만큼 그렇게 이질적인 것이
　　　 아니야.
　　 B: 그것이 사실이라면 동전에 양면이 있듯이 다른 면이 없이는 발
　　　 전할 수 없겠지.
해설_ progress 진행하다, 발전하다
어휘_ prospect 전망 process 과정
정답_ (d)

16.

해석_ A: Marx와 Simmel 모두 갈등을 사회 체제에 만연되어 있는,
　　　 피할 수 없는 성질이라고 보았지.
　　 B: 나도 동의할 수 있어. 그렇지만 그들 각자의 지적 탐구 목적과
　　　 사회 본성에 대한 가정은 매우 달라.

해설_ Marx와 Simmel에 대해 이야기하고 있는 대화이다. A가
'Marx와 Simmel은 둘 다 갈등은 사회 체제의 불가피한 특징이
라고 봤다'고 얘기하자 B는 이 말에 동의하면서 '하지만(but) 지
적 탐구 목적(intellectual purposes)과 사회 본성에 대한 가
정(assumptions about the nature of society)은 둘이
각각 매우 다르다'는 이야기를 하고 있다. 즉, 빈칸에는 '각각'을
뜻하는 respective가 와야 대화의 흐름이 자연스러워진다.

어휘_ conflict 갈등 assumption 가정 vastly 대단히

정답_ (a)

17.

해석_ A: 공짜 피자 고마워. 콜라도 공짜로 마셔도 돼?
　　　B: 기회를 지나치게 이용하지 마라.

해설_ Don't press your luck. 기회를 지나치게 이용하지 마.

어휘_ squeeze 짜내다 harass 괴롭히다

정답_ (b)

18.

해석_ A: 네게 딱 어울리는데. 사 버려!
　　　B: 나도 그러고 싶은데 나에게는 너무 비싸.

해설_ cannot afford ~할 여유가 없다, 구입할 수 없다

어휘_ suit 어울리다

정답_ (b)

19.

해석_ A: 난 엄마보다 아빠를 닮았어. 넌 어떠니?
　　　B: 난 우리 부모님 둘 다 안 닮았어.

해설_ bear a resemblance 닮다

어휘_ take after 닮다 resemblance 유사

정답_ (b)

20.

해석_ A: 여보, 좀 캐주얼한 옷 없어? 이거 너무 정장인데.
　　　B: 오늘밤은 정식 디너 모임에 가는 거잖아요. 아니에요?

해설_ black-tie dinner 정장 차림을 요하는 디너 파티

어휘_ formal 격식 차린

정답_ (a)

21.

해석_ A: 요즘 젊은이들은 1960년대 우리가 입었던 것과 같은 스타일의
　　　　옷을 입고 다녀.
　　　B: 역사는 반복된다고 하잖아.

해설_ history repeats itself 역사는 반복된다

정답_ (a)

22.

해석_ A: 혼자 도망가려고 하지 마. 잊지 마, 우리가 같은 배를 탔다는 걸.
　　　B: 잔소리 좀 그만해. 나도 내가 어떤 처지인지 알아.

해설_ be on the same boat 한 배를 타다, 같은 처지이다

어휘_ run away 도망치다 by oneself 혼자

정답_ (b)

23.

해석_ A: 그가 사표를 낼까?
　　　B: 글쎄, 편한 자리를 쉽게 포기하지는 않겠지.

해설_ cushy 쉬운, 편한

어휘_ resign 사직하다 give up 포기하다

정답_ (c)

24.

해석_ A: 그 사람에게 절대 술 한 방울도 주지 마.
　　　B: 알아, 그 사람 알코올 중독자잖아.

해설_ compulsive drinker 알코올 중독자(alcoholic)

어휘_ comprehensive 포괄적인

정답_ (a)

25.

해석_ A: 우리는 화성을 인간이 살기에 완벽한 곳으로 만들 수 있지. 화
　　　　성의 대기를 변화시킬 필요가 있지만 아이러니하게도 오염이
　　　　화성엔 약이 되지.
　　　B: 화성을 오염시키는 것은 큰 문제가 안 될 거야. 우리가 지금 지
　　　　구에서 하고 있는 것이니.

해설_ medicine 약

어휘_ pollution 오염 diseases 질병

정답_ (c)

26.

해석_ 지구에 살아있는 모든 물질들은 오랫동안 다채로운 역사를 나눈다.
　　　우리의 별은 45억 년 전 소용돌이에서 태어났다. 그리고 이후 6억
　　　년 동안의 변함없는 원시 물질들의 충돌은 지표면을 살 수 없는 곳
　　　으로 만들었다.

해설_ uninhabitable 사람이 살 수 없는

어휘_ maelstrom 큰 소용돌이 bombardment 충격
　　　primordial 원시의 debris 파편, 잔해

정답_ (a)

27.

해석_ 경찰은 지난 10일 동안 상당한 분량의 자료들을 모았었다고 소식통은 전한다.

해설_ accumulate 축적하다, 모으다

어휘_ considerable 상당한

정답_ (b)

28.

해석_ 2004년 수정안들은 경찰이 치안판사에게 경찰이 정보를 확인하는 동안 시계를 멈출 수 있는 즉, "Dead Time"을 요구하는 것을 허용한다.

어휘_ amendment 수정안 magistrate 치안판사 grant 승인하다 surveillance 감시, 감독

정답_ (c)

29.

해석_ Law Council과 인권 운동가들은 연장된 구금에 대하여 반테러 권력(즉, 법규)의 남용이라고 비난하였다.

해설_ abuse 남용

어휘_ detention 구금 council 회의 libertarian 자유론자 consensus (의견) 일치 contention 투쟁, 싸움

정답_ (b)

30.

해석_ 경찰은 (주차) 문제를 바로잡기 위해서 이 지역에서 불법 주차 단속을 확고히 하고 있다.

해설_ tighten 강화하다

어휘_ rectify 수정하다 suppress 억압하다 stir 고무하다 exert 행사하다

정답_ (a)

31.

해석_ 각각의 승무원들은 개개인이 화장실 도구를 가지고 있다. 승무원들은 또한 호수에 달린 개인 소변 깔때기를 가지고 있어서 소변은 오물통에 저장되어진다.

해석_ deposit 저장하다

어휘_ urine 소변 mature 숙성시키다 contain 담다

정답_ (b)

32.

해석_ 인간과 유인원을 더 다르게 하는 것은 척추가 엉치에 연결된 장소의 위치이다.

해설_ attach 붙다

어휘_ differentiate A from B A와 B를 구별하다 spine 척추 subscribe 동의하다, 서명하다 incline 기울어지다

정답_ (b)

33.

해석_ 건국의 아버지들의 시대로부터 시작해서 산업혁명 시기와 두 차례의 세계대전을 겪으면서 미국인들은 말 그대로 다른 나라들을 엄청나게 압도했다.

해설_ tower over는 '~을 압도하다'는 의미이다.

어휘_ founding father (국가 · 제도 · 시설 · 운동의) 창립자, 미국 헌법 제정자 industrial revolution 산업혁명

정답_ (c)

34.

해석_ 스트레스가 없게 하기 위해서, 우리는 명상의 시간을 가진다는 것은 중요하다. 그것은 마음을 정화하고, 새로운 날을 시작하게 만들어 준다.

해설_ reflection 명상

어휘_ clear out minds 마음을 정화하다

정답_ (a)

35.

해석_ James는 요리 솜씨로 유명하다. 하지만 오늘의 게 요리는 정말 맛이 끔찍했다.

해설_ culinary skill은 '요리 솜씨'라는 뜻이다.

어휘_ crab 게 awful 맛이 너무 형편없는 culinary 부엌의, 요리의

정답_ (a)

36.

해석_ 그 정치적 음모 때문에 민주당은 클린턴 정부에 책임이 있다고 주장했다.

해설_ liability는 '책임'이란 뜻이다.

어휘_ conspiracy 음모 insist on 주장하다 impediment 방해물 corrodibility 부패 가능성

정답_ (a)

37.

해석_ 선거에 이기기 위해 그들은 일련의 전술을 사용했다.

해설_ employ (물건, 수단 등을) 사용하다

어휘_ in order to do ~하기 위해 election 선거 tactic 전술
possess 소유하다(possessed는 '뭔가에 홀린, 열중한' 이라
는 뜻이 되기도 함)

정답_ (c)

38.

해석_ 현지 법률회사와 균형 잡힌 관계를 찾는 미국 법률회사와는 달리
영국 법률회사는 전면적 접근으로 현지 회사의 장악을 시도한다.

해설_ dominate 장악하다, 재배하다

어휘_ firm 회사 regional 지역의 full-fledged 충분히 발달된,
완전한, 철저한 approach 접근

정답_ (b)

39.

해석_ 계약 위반이 없는 한, 논쟁거리가 다시 되지는 않을 것이다.

해설_ debate 논쟁, 토론

어휘_ rekindle 다시 불을 붙이다 breach of contract 계약 위반

정답_ (d)

40.

해석_ John은 멍청하고 게으르지만 그래도 늘 그녀의 절친한 친구일 거
라고 그녀가 말하자 John은 엄청 화가 났다.

해설_ 문맥상 was _________는 '엄청 화가 났다' 는 의미가 되어야 한
다. 따라서 빈칸에는 '엄청나게 화난' 이란 뜻의 incensed가 적
절하다. 기본형 incense는 '~를 매우 화나게 하다' 는 의미의 동
사이다.

어휘_ enrapture 황홀하게 하다 invigorate 상쾌하게 하다

정답_ (a)

41.

해석_ 진화론은 우리 사회에 만연해 있다. 그리고 기독교인들은 어떻게
이런 가르침에 대처하고 무신론자들에게 그들의 믿음을 다시 생각
하게 만들지에 대한 도전이 필요하다.

해설_ Darwinism 진화론

어휘_ pervasive 퍼지는, 스며드는 Creationism 창조론

정답_ (b)

42.

해석_ Rice와 Gheit는 미국과 이집트 상호간의 이익에 관한 주제를 토
론했다.

해설_ mutual 상호적인

어휘_ ambiguous 모호한, 분명하지 않은 vague 애매한, 막연한

정답_ (a)

43.

해석_ 피부가 태양에 직접적 노출이 잦을수록 피부암의 가능성은 높아
진다.

해설_ expose 노출하다

어휘_ frequently 빈번하게 possibility 가능성 skin cancer
피부암 increase 증가하다

정답_ (a)

44.

해석_ 오늘 밤 이 작전의 최종 목적지는 인천이다.

해설_ operation 작전

어휘_ final destination 최종 목적지 association 결사

정답_ (d)

45.

해석_ 그들은 모두 부패 기업의 유산은 혼돈과 파산과 절망이라는 데 동
의했다.

해설_ that 이하는 부패한 기업이 물려주는 것이라곤 혼돈과 파산과 절
망이라는 의미의 문장이다. 따라서 '대를 이어 물려주는 것', 즉
'유산' 이란 의미의 legacy가 빈칸에 적절하다. 만일 (b)가
bequest(유증)였다면 역시 답이 될 수 있었을 것이다.

어휘_ corrupt 부패한 chaos 혼돈 bankruptcy 파산 despair
절망 penance 참회

정답_ (c)

46.

해석_ ELS는 현재와 미래의 환경 요구에 적합한 가장 적절한 해결책 제
공에 기여하는 환경 문제 해결 팀입니다.

해설_ dedicated 헌신적인

어휘_ demand 요구

정답_ (a)

47.

해석_ 우리는 회사의 재정을 튼튼히 하고, 우리의 고객들에게 신뢰성을
부여하고, 현재와 미래의 직원들이 전문성을 기를 수 있는 기회를
주려고 전력을 기울이고 있습니다.

해설_ committed 헌신적인, 전념하는

어휘_ dependability 의존 가능성, 신뢰성 mitigate 완화하다
creolize 혼합시키다

정답_ (a)

48.

해석_ 천체의 남극점 부분의 은하수의 일부분은 보이지 않거나 미국에서
는 관찰 가능할 만큼 높이 떠오르지도 않는다.

해설_ vicinity 근처 (남극점의 '근처'가 되어야 자연스러우므로
vicinity가 적절)

어휘_ Milky Way 은하수 celestial pole 천체의 극

정답_ (a)

49.

해석_ 많은 사람들이 어떤 음식에 대해 좋지 않은 반응을 나타내고 있지
만 진정한 음식 알레르기는 면역 시스템에 의한 반응이다.

해설_ trigger 유발하다, 방아쇠를 당기다

어휘_ reaction 반응 immune system 면역 체계

정답_ (d)

50.

해석_ 중국 정부는 새로운 지도자 선출을 담당하는 800명의 선거인단 인
원을 늘리는 양보안들을 내놓았지만 반대파들은 그 제안들은 충분
하지 않다며 반발하고 있다.

해설_ concession 양보

어휘_ allowance 용돈 agreement 일치, 협정

정답_ (a)

Final Test (2)

1.

해석_ A: 나 남자친구랑 헤어졌어. 난 지금은 솔로야.

　　　B: 안됐다. 그 남자는 좋은 사람이라고 생각했는데.

해설_ 애인이 없는 상태의 사람을 single이라고 표현한다.

어휘_ break up with ~와 헤어지다

정답_ (a)

2.

해석_ A: 그들은 자동차 사고로 죽었다고 들었어요. 어떻게 된 거예요?

　　　B: 자동차들이 충돌해서 불이 났고 그들은 타죽었어요.

해설_ be incinerated 불에 타다

어휘_ be extinguished (불이) 진화되다 be executed 처형되다

　　　be discarded 처분되다

정답_ (b)

3.

해석_ A: 아빠! 이 돌은 참 이상한 모양을 하고 있어요.

　　　B: 아마도 천장에서 떨어지는 물에 부식되었나 보다.

해설_ be eroded 부식되다

어휘_ melt 녹이다 cut 자르다, 베다 dissolve 용해하다

정답_ (d)

4.

해석_ A: 법정에서 "So help you God"라고 하는 게 무슨 의민지
알아?

　　　B: 응, 아마도 "So help you God"라는 말은 "Let God
help you do so"(신이 진실을 말하도록 도움을 주다)란 말
로 쉽게 풀이할 수 있지.

해설_ paraphrase 쉽게 풀어서 설명하다

어휘_ composite 합성하다 prose 산문체로 쓰다 article 도제
계약을 하다

정답_ (d)

5.

해석_ A: 우리가 그 시장에서 그 제품을 철수해야 하는 주된 이유가 뭐
죠?

　　　B: 기본적으로 한국의 군수 시장은 너무 작아져서 경제적으로 실
용적인 생산량을 유지하기가 어렵게 되었습니다.

해설_ production run 생산 가동

어휘_ withdraw 철수하다, 물러나다 defense market 군수 시장

sustain 유지하다   viable 생존 가능성이 있는

정답_ (c)

6.

해석_ A: '위원회'의 철자가 어떻게 되니?

B: 잘 모르겠는 걸. 찾아봐 줄게. 여기 있다. 이 단어에는 'm' 자가 2개, 't' 자가 2개, 'e' 자가 2개 들어가네.

해설_ look up 찾아보다

어휘_ committee 위원회

정답_ (b)

7.

해석_ A: 그 여자는 예뻐지기 위해서 뭐든지 다 했어.

B: 알아, 코 모양 바꾸려고 성형수술까지 했잖아.

해설_ plastic surgery 성형수술

어휘_ pharyngeal surgery 후두 수술   hemorrhoidectomy 치질 수술   kidney transplant 신장 이식

정답_ (c)

8.

해석_ A: 그래, 좋은 점수를 받았다면서! 놀라운 소식이구나. 내가 너희 집에 갈때까지 넌 시험 준비를 안 했는데.

B: 맞아, 하지만 며칠 전에 벼락치기를 했지.

해설_ studying과 preparing 역시 틀린 단어는 아니다. 그러나 문맥의 의미상 cramming(벼락치기하다)이 가장 적절한 답이다.

어휘_ peer 엿보다, 훔쳐보다

정답_ (b)

9.

해석_ A: Robert와 Sam은 정말 자기들밖에 모르는 사람들이야.

B: 나도 완전히 동의해.

해설_ egotistic 자기중심적인 (여기서 share는 공통된 특성을 가진다는 의미임)

어휘_ arrogant 거만한   elegant 우아한

정답_ (a)

10.

해석_ A: 시합이 굉장히 힘들었는데, Sam이 결국 성공해서 일등상을 탔어.

B: 좋은 소식인데!

해설_ pull it off는 하려고 시도하는 일(what you are trying to do)을 '성공해내다(succeed)' 는 의미로 쓰는 숙어 표현이다.

어휘_ competition 경쟁, 대회   eventually 결국, 마침내

정답_ (c)

11.

해석_ A: 너는 속임수를 썼어. 네 테니스 라켓이 내 것보다 크잖아.

B: 비겁한 패배자가 되지 말라고. 이것은 단지 게임일 뿐이야.

해설_ Don't be (such) a sore loser. 비겁한 패배자가 되지 마라.

어휘_ cheat 부정행위를 하다, 반칙을 쓰다

정답_ (d)

12.

해석_ A: Jones (의사) 선생님이 네가 다쳤을 때 너의 상처를 치료해줬니?

B: 그럼. 그는 날 잘 돌봐주었어.

해설_ '상처를 치유하다' 라는 의미로는 treat를 쓴다. cure는 질병 등을 치료할 때 쓴다.

어휘_ scar 상처

정답_ (c)

13.

해석_ A: 태양을 봐. 완전 용광로야.

B: 여기, 자외선 차단제 좀 발라. 이거 무지하게 강한 거야.

해설_ 날씨가 너무 더워서 "완전 용광로 같다."고 할 때는 It's like a furnace. 또는 It's a furnace.라고 쓴다. furnace는 '보일러' 또는 '용광로' 를 뜻하는 단어이다.

어휘_ put on (화장품 등을) 바르다(동작)   sun block 자외선 차단제   extra strong 무지하게 강한(extra는 형용사나 부사 앞에서 형용사를 강조해주는 역할을 함)   primitive 원시적인   heat 열   taciturn 과묵한, 말수가 적은

정답_ (c)

14.

해석_ A: 먼저 일을 하고 너의 급료에 대해 우리 한번 이야기해 보자.

B: 이봐, 난 그런 말을 들을 정도로 바보가 아니야.

해설_ I wasn't born yesterday. 난 그런 말을 들을 정도로 바보가 아니야. (어제 태어난 갓난아기처럼 세상물정을 모르는 것이 아니라는 뜻)

어휘_ discuss 의논하다   pay 임금, 급료

정답_ (b)

15.

해석_ A: 아파트는 깨끗이 청소됐어.

B: 벌써? 정말로 지저분했었는데.

해설_ 문맥상 첫 번째 대사는 아파트가 깨끗하게 다 치워졌다는 의미가
되어야 한다. 따라서 빈칸에는 어떤 일을 '꼼꼼하게' 한다고 할 때
쓰이는 **meticulously**가 적절하다.

어휘_ **debonairly** 겸손하게 **putridly** 냄새나게 **determinately**
결정적으로

정답_ (d)

16.

해석_ A: 이 구직자를 채용하는 것을 고려해봐야 하나요?

B: 나 역시도 확신이 없네. 그는 전과자야. 5년간 감옥에 있었지.

해설_ **ex-convict** 전과자

어휘_ **consider** 고려하다 **applicant** 지원자

정답_ (b)

17.

해석_ A: 대학 입학 시험에 붙고 싶어? 그럼 열심히 공부해!

B: 물론 공부를 하죠. 하지만 공부만 하고 놀지 않으면 바보가 된다
고요.

해설_ **dull** 우둔한

어휘_ **pass** (시험에) 합격하다 **entrance exam** 입학 시험
dummy 가짜의, 모조의 **disable** 불구가 되게 만들다

정답_ (c)

18.

해석_ A: 어젯밤에 나는 로또에 당첨되는 꿈을 꿨어

B: 정말? 당첨 숫자가 몇 번인데?

해설_ 문맥상 '꿈을 꿨다'는 의미의 **dreamed**가 가장 적절하다.

어휘_ **lull** 잠을 재우다 **sleek** 윤기가 나다

정답_ (d)

19.

해석_ A: 너의 답은 정답 근처에도 못 갔어. 그건 그냥 지레짐작인 것 같
은데.

B: 정답은 뭔데?

해설_ **whistle in the dark** 지레짐작

어휘_ **dark** 암흑

정답_ (b)

20.

해석_ A: 골동품상 주인이 그러는데 이 그림은 굉장히 귀한 것이래. 값이
얼마인지조차 얘기 못 하더라.

B: 오, 분명히 귀한 물건이겠군.

해설_ **priceless** 값을 따질 수 없이 귀한

어휘_ **valueless** 가치 없는 **costless** 비용이 들지 않는
accountable 책임이 있는

정답_ (b)

21.

해석_ A: 나는 멕시코 여행에 보너스를 쓸 거야.

B: 만일의 경우를 대비해서 돈도 모아놔야 할 걸.

해설_ **save/have something for a rainy day** 만약의 사태에
대비해 ~를 모아두다/준비해두다

정답_ (c)

22.

해석_ A: Jenny가 15,000달러의 장학금을 탔어.

B: 그럴 줄 알았어. 그 앤 늘 그렇게 끈기가 있는 학생이었지.

해설_ **tenacious** 끈기 있는

어휘_ **scholarship** 장학금 **volatile** 증발하기 쉬운 **fraternal**
형제다운 **dull** 머리가 둔한

정답_ (c)

23.

해석_ A: 그만 말해! 난 더 이상 당신의 거짓말을 참을 수가 없어.

B: 난 사실을 말하고 있는 거라고!

해설_ 모두 '참다'의 뜻을 가진 동사(구)이지만, 이 중 **up with**와 어울
려 '참다, 인내하다'는 의미가 되는 동사는 **put**이다. **put up
with**로 통째 외워둘 것.

정답_ (c)

24.

해석_ A: 내가 농담으로 한 말을 Sonny는 너무 심각하게 받아들였어.

B: 그는 그런 농담엔 좀 민감해.

해설_ **susceptible** 받아 들이는, 쉽게 상처를 받는

어휘_ **scrupulous** 견실한, 용의주도한 **insufficient** 부족한
inadequate 부적당한

정답_ (b)

25.

해석_ A: 만약 그들이 우리를 저녁식사에 초대하면 어떻게 할까?

B: 모르겠어. 봐서 되는 대로.

해설_ **play it by ear** 즉흥적으로 대응하다

정답_ (a)

26.

해석_ 만약 당신의 친구와 가족이 뚱뚱해진다면 당신 역시 뚱뚱해질 가능성이 있다. 이런 결론은, 비만은 사회적으로 전염성이 있어서 사람과 사람들 사이에 쉽게 퍼져 나갈 수 있다는 놀랄 만한 새로운 연구를 수행한 연구자들이 내린 것이다.

해설_ fat에서 근거를 찾을 수 있다. 빈칸에는 '비만'을 뜻하는 obesity가 적절.

어휘_ socially 사회적으로 contagious 전염성의 contamination 오염

정답_ (a)

27.

해석_ 영국은 가축으로 만든 제품의 수출을 금지하고 소, 양, 염소 그리고 돼지의 이동을 정지시켰다.

해설_ 빈칸 뒤에 오는 cattle, sheep, goats, and pigs로 정답이 가축(livestock)임을 유추할 수 있다.

어휘_ ban 금지하다 halt 정지시키다

정답_ (c)

28.

해석_ 정보 누설이 허용되지 않았기 때문에 익명을 요구한 한 공무원은 Karbala에서 약 3시간 뒤에 또 하나의 충돌이 일어났다고 말했다.

해설_ on condition of anonymity 익명을 요구한

어휘_ authorized 권한이 있는

정답_ (d)

29.

해석_ 어린 아이들에게는 배꼽(belly button, navel, umbilicus)은 생명의 엄청난 신비 중의 하나이다.

해설_ 동의어를 묻는 문제이다. 빈칸에는 해부학 용어인 umbilicus와 의미가 동일한 navel(배꼽)이 와야 한다.

어휘_ umbilicus 배꼽 mystery 수수께끼

정답_ (a)

30.

해석_ 하와이의 한 남자가 회수 대상이었던 캔에 담긴 칠리를 먹은 후 보툴리누스 중독 증상으로 병원에 입원했다.

해설_ 모두 흔한 질병의 이름들이다. 문장의 내용상 '보툴리누스 중독'을 뜻하는 botulism이 정답.

어휘_ malnutrition 영양실조 epidemic 전염병 diabetes 당뇨병

정답_ (a)

31.

해석_ 월트 디즈니 사는 가족 관련 영화에 더 이상 담배를 피우는 모습은 없을 것이라고 수요일에 발표했다. 이로써 월트 디즈니 사는 흡연 장면을 금지한 헐리웃 사상 최초의 영화사가 되는 것이다.

해설_ depiction은 사진이나 그림 등의 '묘사'를 의미한다. 참고로 '설명'이란 뜻으로도 쓰인다.

어휘_ explanation 설명 elucidation 해명 exposition 박람회

정답_ (b)

32.

해석_ 조사 결과 9명의 경찰관이 잘못된 정보를 제공하는 실수에 대한 책임이 있음이 밝혀졌다.

해설_ hold someone accountable ~에게 책임을 지우다

어휘_ probe 조사 officer 경찰관 be at fault in ~에 대한 책임이 있다 searchable 수색할 수 있는 conductible 전도성 amicable 우호적인

정답_ (d)

33.

해석_ 자신의 직업을 싫어하는 사람이 많은 이유 중에서 중요한 것은 "지루하기" 때문이라고 이 연구에서는 밝혔다.

해설_ specify는 '명확하게 밝히다'라는 뜻이다.

어휘_ boredom 지루함 condemn 비난하다 criticize 비평하다

정답_ (d)

34.

해석_ 인도네시아 의사들은 한 자바 마을에서 8명을 죽이고 22명을 감염시킨 알려지지 않은 질병의 출현을 조사하고 있다.

해설_ outbreak (전쟁 · 질병 등의) 발발, (분노의) 폭발

어휘_ investigate 조사하다 infect 감염시키다 contamination 오염 disease 질병 entrance 입장

정답_ (c)

35.

해석_ 한국에서는 여성들이 각 분야의 직업에 종사하고 있지만 정치적으로 지도적인 역할은 최근까지만 해도 여성에게는 금지된 분야였다.

해설_ off는 떨어져 있다는 의미를 내포하고 있는 어휘로 off limits라고 하면 '출입 금지인'의 의미로 쓰이는 표현이다. 어디에 출입 금지인지 밝히고 싶을 때는 off limits to 뒤에 장소나 대상을 밝히면 된다.

어휘_ labor force 노동 인력 obstacle 장애 filter 여과기 leadership role 지도자직

정답_ (a)

36.

해석_ 음식을 먹는 것 같은 행동을 다른 사람이 관찰한다면 그런 행동을 담당하는 뇌의 부분이 자극을 받을 수 있는 가능성도 있다.

해설_ **be stimulated** 자극되다

어휘_ **plausible** 그럴싸한, 진실 같은 **correspond** ~에 반응하다

정답_ (c)

37.

해석_ 중국 경찰은 가짜 약을 만들어 국내와 해외에 판매한 일당들을 수색하면서 1톤의 가짜 비아그라 약을 몰수했다.

해설_ _____ **drugs**는 문맥상 앞서 나온 가짜 비아그라(fake Viagra)와 대구를 이루는 '가짜 약물' 이 되어어야겠다. 보기 중 '가짜' 를 뜻하는 형용사는 **counterfeit**이다.

어휘_ **seize** 몰수하다 **pharmaceutical** 제약의

정답_ (b)

38.

해석_ 아이러니하게 세계에 성인 책을 소개한 보수적인 나라의 학교들은 인간의 번식이라는 주제에 대해 젊은 학생들에게 가르치는 것을 회피했다.

해설_ **ironically**에서 힌트를 얻을 수 있다. 성인 책을 소개한 것에 모순되는 것을 뜻하기 위해선 '보수적인' 이 자연스럽다.

어휘_ **reproduction** 번식 **progressive** 진보적인 **meticulous** 세심한, 꼼꼼한

정답_ (b)

39.

해석_ 우레와 같은 폭발음과 이후에 연기가 하늘로 솟구치면서 불길은 땅 위에 퍼졌다.

해설_ **billow**의 주어가 될 단어는 **smoke**밖에 없다. 나머지는 적절치 않다. **billow**는 '파도치다, 소용돌이치다, 밀려오다, 부풀게 하다' 의 뜻이다.

어휘_ **missile** 미사일 **bullet** 총알

정답_ (b)

40.

해석_ 미국 대중의 참을성이 점점 옅어지면서 병력의 축소를 요구하고 있는 의원들의 숫자가 많아지고 있다.

해설_ 마음이나 심경의 변화로 주장이 기운이 약해질 때는 **wear thin**을 쓴다.

어휘_ **press for** ~에 대해 압력을 넣다, 강하게 주장하다

정답_ (c)

41.

해석_ 샌프란시스코 시장은 시 직원들에게 수돗물이 사용 가능할 때는 시 자금으로 생수를 구매하는 것을 금지했다.

해설_ **tap water** 수돗물

어휘_ **mayor** 시장 **ban** 금지하다 **subterranean** 지하수 **pond** 연못 **plumb** (절망, 비참함 등과 같이 좋지 않은) 감정의 늪에 빠지다

정답_ (d)

42.

해석_ 여성 응답자들의 48.5%가 정기적으로 약물을 복용하는 반면, 남자들은 34.4%가 복용하는 것으로 보아 여성이 약물에 보다 더 중독이 잘 된다는 것을 알 수 있었다.

해설_ **be addicted to** ~에 중독되다

어휘_ **respondent** 응답자 **take drugs** 약물을 복용하다 **on a regular basis** 정기적으로 **vulnerable** 저항력이 없는, 취약한 **favourable** 좋다고 생각하는 **inevitable** 불가피한, 필수적인

정답_ (b)

43.

해석_ 수백 명의 시위자들이 이슬람 사원 밖에서 경찰과 부딪쳤고 해산하기 전까지 수 시간동안 사원을 점거했다.

해설_ **be dispersed** 뿔뿔이 흩어지다

어휘_ **demonstrator** 시위자 **clash** 충돌하다 **mosque** 이슬람 사원 **occupy** 차지하다

정답_ (c)

44.

해석_ 엄청난 몬순 비가 60만 명을 난민으로 만든 돌발적인 홍수 때문에 인도 군인과 민간인 구호 팀은 아셈 주 동북부에서 대기하고 있다.

해설_ **heavy monsoon**에서 힌트를 얻을 수 있다. 장마가 홍수를 '유발' 하였으므로 **trigger**가 적절하다.

어휘_ **flood** 홍수 **monsoon** 몬순, 장마

정답_ (b)

45.

해석_ 러시아 정부가 **Litvinenko** 사건의 살인 용의자의 인도를 거부하자 영국에서 축출된 4명의 러시아 외교관들이 영국을 떠났다.

해설 stand-off 대치, 교착

어휘 extradite 송환하다

정답 (b)

46.

해석 의장과 부의장의 부재 시, 감독관은 두 사람의 의무와 책임의 지위를 맡는다.

해설 assume은 '지위를 맡다'라는 뜻을 가지고 있다.

어휘 duty 의무 responsibility 책임

정답 (b)

47.

해석 지역 카지노에서 거액의 돈을 가지고 달아난 강도는 금요일 오전 현재 여전히 도망 중이다.

해설 make off 달아나다

어휘 gunman 무장 강도 put off 연기하다, 미루다

정답 (b)

48.

해석 혁명의 광풍이 러시아를 휩쓸던 1917년에 왕의 자리에서 물러난 러시아 황제 니콜라스 2세는 결국 수감되었다.

해설 Czar(황제)와 revolutionary로 추측할 수 있다. 혁명이 일어나고 황제가 물러났다는 표현이 문맥상 적절하므로 '사임시키다'의 뜻인 abdicate이 정답이다.

어휘 revolutionary 혁명적인 fervor 열정 detain 감금하다

정답 (a)

49.

해석 보고서는 우주인들에 의한 알콜 섭취에 대하여 다루었다. 그 보고서는 우주 비행사 중 두 명이 취해 있었다고 말한다.

해설 alcohol에서 힌트를 찾을 수 있다. intoxicated는 '술에 취한'이란 뜻이다.

어휘 astronaut 우주 비행사

정답 (d)

50.

해석 케이프 코드의 한 남자가 배심원 의무를 피하기 위해서 자신을 동성애 혐오자, 인종 차별주의자, 습관적 거짓말쟁이라고 주장하자, 판사가 화가 나서 이 남자의 기소 여부를 검찰에 의뢰했다.

해설 jury duty에서 힌트를 얻을 수 있다. 배심원 의무 회피를 위해 거짓말을 한 것에 대한 조치로써 검사들에게 기소 가능한 죄목을 알아보라고 회부한 것이다. 따라서 경찰(police)보다는 판사(judge)가 적절하다.

어휘 homophobic 동성애 혐오자 judge 판사 prosecutor 검사

정답 (d)

Final Test (3)

1.

해석_ **A:** 레이저 광선은 위험해. 너는 사람을 그것으로 실명시킬 수 있어.

　　B: 걱정하지 마. 나는 그것으로 어떤 사람의 눈도 가리키지 않을 거야.

해설_ **go blind** 장님이 되다

어휘_ **blind** 눈이먼 **dangerous** 위험한

정답_ **(b)**

2.

해석_ **A:** 왜 그런지는 모르겠는데, 오늘은 지금까지 한 일들이 다 재앙이었어.

　　B: 아마도 오늘 아침 꿈자리가 사나워서 그랬을 거야.

해설_ **get up on the wrong side of (the) bed** 아침부터 기운이 사납다, 꿈자리가 나쁘다

어휘_ **cradle** 요람 **layer** 층

정답_ **(b)**

3.

해석_ **A:** 네 성적표를 네 어머니가 보셨을 때 화를 냈니?

　　B: 그래, 완전히 폭발하셨어.

해설_ **blow a fuse** 몹시 화내다

어휘_ **report card** 성적표

정답_ **(a)**

4.

해석_ **A:** 안내 광고에 난 비서 자리 때문에 전화 드렸는데요.

　　B: 죄송해요. 이미 찼습니다.

해설_ **sorry**와 **already**로 유추해 보아 자리가 이미 ‘찼다’는 뜻의 단어가 와야 함을 알 수 있다.

어휘_ **secretarial** 비서의

정답_ **(a)**

5.

해석_ **A:** 우리 형이 전부 A를 맞았어.

　　B: 전혀 놀랍지 않아. 그는 아주 부지런한 학생이잖아.

해설_ **straight A’s** 전과목 A

어휘_ **diligent** 근면한

정답_ **(b)**

6.

해석_ **A:** 너는 그녀가 그 일을 혼자 하게 내버려둬야 돼. 만약 네가 도우려고 한다면 그녀는 화를 낼 거야.

　　B: 알아. 나는 정말로 그녀의 화를 돋우기 싫어.

해설_ **step on someone’s toes** 화를 돋우다

어휘_ **be offended** 기분이 상하다 **ladder** 사다리

정답_ **(d)**

7.

해석_ **A:** 이미 난 돌이킬 수 없는 강을 건넌 것 같아. 그녀에게 이미 난 다른 사람을 만나고 있다고 말했어.

　　B: 그렇게 말한 게 잘한 일 같지는 않다.

해설_ **burn one’s bridges** 배수의 진을 치다

어휘_ **see someone** 누군가와 교제하고 있다, 누군가와 사귀고 있다

정답_ **(d)**

8.

해석_ **A:** 난 정말로 Amanda랑 데이트를 하고 싶어.

　　B: 글쎄, 그녀를 기분 좋게 해줘서 그녀가 널 좋아하게 만들어봐.

해설_ **curry favor with someone** ~의 비위를 맞추다, ~에게 알랑거리다

어휘_ **hamper** 훼방하다 **shield** 보호하다

정답_ **(a)**

9.

해석_ **A:** 만약에 영업 관리자가 되고 싶다면 협상 중에 요구나 거절을 잘해야 해.

　　B: 아빠, 좋은 충고 감사해요.

해설_ **drive a hard bargain** 유리한 거래를 하다

어휘_ **advice** 조언

정답_ **(a)**

10.

해석_ **A:** 휴가는 어떻게 보냈어?

　　B: 최고였어. 난 카지노에서 대박을 냈어. 500달러를 벌었어.

해설_ **go to town** (크게) 성공하다, 돈에 구애받지 않고 마음껏 하다

어휘_ **pub** 술집

정답_ **(a)**

11.

해석_ **A:** 이 보고서 작업을 밤새 해야 할 것 같다.

　　B: 그러면 커피를 좀 끓여두는 것이 좋겠다.

해설_ **coffee**를 끓인다는 표현에는 **brew**가 쓰인다.

어휘_ **broil** (고기, 생선 따위를) 굽다 **brand** 상표
breed 새끼를 낳다

정답_ (a)

12.

해석_ A: 우린 가능한 한 빨리 이 남자를 잡아야 해.

B: 유감입니다만, 그의 행방에 대한 단서가 전혀 없습니다.

해설_ 문맥상 '단서, 실마리'를 뜻하는 **clue**가 적절하다.

어휘_ **catch hold of** ~을 잡다 **whereabouts** 소재(지) **glue** 풀 **slew** 습지, 늪

정답_ (b)

13.

해석_ A: 발이 부어서 너무 아파.

B: 이런, 안됐구나. 앞으로 일주일간은 제대로 못 걷겠는걸.

해설_ **swelling** 증대, 팽창

어휘_ **clearing** 제거 **steering** 조종

정답_ (a)

14.

해석_ A: 난 그가 입양이란 사실을 몰랐었어.

B: 그래. 그 가여운 애는 자기 친부모에 대해 아무것도 몰랐어.

해설_ **biological**은 '생물학적인'이란 뜻으로, '낳아준 부모', 즉 '친부모'를 영어로는 **biological parents**라고 한다.

어휘_ **adopted child** 입양아 **chemical** 화학의 **regional** 지역의 **political** 정치적인

정답_ (b)

15.

해석_ A: 그 반란군들이 갑자기 무기를 버리고 정부에 굴복하다니 놀라워.

B: 글쎄, 난 그렇게 생각 안 해. 쌍방이 비밀리에 협상을 해서 밀약했다는 소문이 있어.

해설_ **cloaked in mystery** 의문에 가려진

어휘_ **insurgent** 폭도 **stoke** 불을 지피다 **soak** 젖게 하다

정답_ (d)

16.

해석_ A: 대학은 수업료만 부담하는 부분 장학금을 주고 있어요.

B: 그럼, 누가 당신 경비의 나머지를 지불해 줄 거죠?

해설_ B의 대사에서 **the rest of your expenses**를 보아 부분 장학금이라는 내용을 추론할 수 있다. 따라서 '부분적인'이란 의미의

partial이 정답이다.

정답_ (c)

17.

해석_ A: 정부에서 제시한 이 법안은 완전히 헌법에 위배되잖아.

B: 그래, 하지만 정부는 언제나 수적 우세를 이용해서 헌법을 개정할 수 있으니까 이 법안을 의회에 통과시킬 수 있지.

해설_ **constitution**(헌법)에서 힌트를 얻을 수 있다. 헌법을 '개정'한다고 할 때에는 **amend**가 쓰인다.

어휘_ **constitution** 헌법 **parliament** 의회 **mend** 고치다, 수선하다, (환자를) 고치다

정답_ (b)

18.

해석_ A: 숲속에서 강가를 따라서 우리가 산책하곤 했던 저녁시간들을 기억하니?

B: 그럼. 난 아직 너와 함께 보냈던 옛 기억들을 간직하고 있어.

해설_ **cherish** 마음에 간직하다

어휘_ **nourish** ~에 자양분을 주다, 기르다, 조성하다

정답_ (a)

19.

해석_ A: 그에게 불평해 봤자야. 그는 자신의 팀을 전혀 통제할 수 없다고.

B: 그게 바로 사람들이 그를 이빨 빠진 호랑이라고 부르는 이유야.

해설_ (b)의 **spent**는 형용사로 '힘이 빠져 버린'의 뜻으로 쓰였다.

어휘_ **professional** 전문가

정답_ (b)

20.

해석_ A: 이번으로 나는 두 번째로 국가 팀에 선발되지 못했어.

B: 넌 다음에 다시 시도할 기회가 있고, 그리고 여전히 후배들을 코치할 수 있으니까 그렇게 낙담하지 마. 그리고 밝은 면을 바라보고 미래에 대해서 좀 더 긍정적이 되어봐.

해설_ **look on the bright side** 낙관적으로 보다, 긍정적인 면을 보다

어휘_ **be selected** 선발되다

정답_ (d)

21.

해석_ A: 전 이번 모임을 돌파 작전 회의라고 부르고 싶군요.

B: 정말입니다. 전 우리가 제기했던 각기 다른 사안들을 중점적으로 다루는 공통적인 정책에 대해서 결국 우리들 모두가 동의하

게 되었다는 점에서 당신의 말에 동의합니다.

해설_ breakthrough 돌파, 약진, 발전

어휘_ policy 정책, 방침 address an issue 문제를 다루다 breakpoint 구분점 break-up 헤어짐, 이별 break time 쉬는 시간

정답_ (a)

22.

해석_ A: 이 사람의 사망 사유를 아십니까?

B: 아직은 모릅니다. 의사들이 아직 시체 부검을 실시하기 전이라서요.

해설_ perform은 '~을 행하다' 는 의미로 perform an autopsy 라고 하면 '부검하다' 는 뜻이 된다.

어휘_ treat 다루다, 대접하다 recover 되찾다 operate 수술하다

정답_ (b)

23.

해석_ A: 그는 자기 돈을 모두 잃고 우울해 하다 자살했어.

B: 그 사람은 분명 모든 희망과 의지를 잃었을 거야.

해설_ bereave - bereft/bereaved - bereft/bereaved ~을 빼앗다 be bereft of ~을 잃다

어휘_ sweep - swept - swept 쓸다 dwell - dwelt - dwelt 살다, 거주하다

정답_ (c)

24.

해석_ A: 새 차 살 계획 있니?

B: 아니. 이제 막 새 집을 샀어. 그래서 새 차를 살 여력이 없어. 아마 내년에는 사겠지.

해설_ afford는 무엇을 구입할 '여유가 되다' 는 의미인데, 주로 can't afford 또는 not be able to afford(~를 살 여유가 없다)와 같이 부정형으로 쓰인다.

어휘_ repair 수리하다 exchange 교환하다

정답_ (b)

25.

해석_ A: 중국의 철학자, 노자가 "도덕경" 이란 책을 썼지. 내가 지금껏 읽어 본 것 중에서 제일 역설적이었어. 읽어 본 적 있니?

B: 그럼. 그건 마치 이해하면서도 동시에 이해하지 않는 것과도 마찬가지야. 다시 말해서, 그건 그 책을 읽으면서도 안 읽는 것과 같단 말이지.

해설_ B의 대화 내용으로 보아 역설적인 내용임을 알 수 있다. 따라서 빈칸에는 '역설적인' 을 뜻하는 paradoxical이 적절하다.

어휘_ at the same time 동시에 in other words 다시 말해, 즉 lengthy 길이가 긴, 장황한

정답_ (a)

26.

해석_ 가정 폭력과 양육 태만은 보고되지 않는 경우가 많다. 이러한 문제들에 대한 사회의 태도가 부부간의 폭력을 거의 (공개적으로) 다뤄지지 않게 하는 역할을 한다.

해설_ conjugal 부부간의

어휘_ patrimonial 세습적인 juvenile 청소년의 counterfeit 위조의

정답_ (d)

27.

해석_ 홍수로 인해 그 마을은 완전히 초토화되었음에도 불구하고 주민들은 절망하지 않고 한 달 안에 마을을 새로이 세웠다.

해설_ despair 절망

어휘_ flexibility 유연성

정답_ (c)

28.

해석_ 그는 처음에는 정직해 보였으나 얼마 지나지 않아서 못미더워 보이는 행동이 문제가 되었다.

해설_ treacherous 불충분한, 믿을 수 없는

어휘_ insidious 교활한 scrupulous 빈틈없는, 꼼꼼한

정답_ (c)

29.

해석_ 포위군으로 둘러싸여 양식을 공급할 수 없게 되자 수비군들은 곧 양식이 다 떨어질까 두려워했다.

해설_ be exhausted 고갈되다

어휘_ be surrounded 포위되다 besieger 포위군 replenish 계속 공급하다 be hoarded 저장되다 superfluous 과잉의 obtainable 입수할 수 있는

정답_ (a)

30.

해석_ 그들의 결혼생활은 심한 폭력과 말싸움으로 얼룩졌기 때문에 순탄치 않았다.

해설_ (be) fraught with ~로 가득 찬, 얼룩진

어휘_ imminent 임박한 obvious 명백한 tranquil 잔잔한

정답_ (b)

31.

해석_ 그녀는 박수 갈채를 받고 기뻐했다. 다른 사람들처럼 칭찬을 받는 것을 좋아했다.

해설_ 명예, 표창을 뜻하는 **accolade**에서 힌트를 얻을 수 있다.

어휘_ **vindicate** 주장하다, 요구하다

정답_ (a)

32.

해석_ 그는 자신이 결코 위대한 작가가 되지 못할 것이라는 사실을 용인하게 되기까지는 오랜 시간이 걸렸다.

해설_ **come to terms with** 굴복하다, 받아들이다

어휘_ **acceptance** 승인 **allowance** 할당액, 용돈 **term** 전문용어

정답_ (d)

33.

해석_ 그는 하얀 쥐 두 마리를 교회로 가져다가 그것들을 바닥에 풀어주었다.

해설_ **let loose** 풀어주다

어휘_ **careless** 부주의한

정답_ (d)

34.

해석_ 정치인들은 대중에 대해 책임을 져야 할 위치에 있기 때문에, 자신을 스캔들로부터 멀어지게 하는 데 많은 관심을 가지고 있다.

해설_ **vested interest** 한 쪽으로 치우친 흥미, 관여, 이해 관계

어휘_ **be held accountable** 책임을 지다 **insulate** 절연하다 **settle** 설치하다 **provoke** 도발하다 **restrict** 제한하다

정답_ (d)

35.

해석_ 경제의 발목을 잡는 높은 소득세는 새로운 투자 자본의 원천을 막아왔다.

해설_ **choke off** 질식시키다

어휘_ **swallow up** 삼키다 **cripple** 불구가 되게 하다

정답_ (c)

36.

해석_ 이러한 언급으로 미루어 당신은 순진하고 세상물정을 모르는 사람이겠군요.

해설_ **ingenuous** 천진난만한

어휘_ **remark** 언급, 논평 **unaware of** ~을 모르는 **reality** 실재, 현실 **stimulating** 고무적인 **wily** 교활한

정답_ (d)

37.

해석_ 훌륭한 스포츠 정신은 비록 의견이 다르다 할지라도 심판의 판정에 승복할 것을 요구한다.

해설_ **concur with** ~에 동의하다

어휘_ **sportsmanship** 스포츠 정신, 운동가 정신 **umpire** 심판(**judge**라고도 함) **even if** 설령 ~라 할지라도

정답_ (a)

38.

해석_ 소아마비는 거의 사라졌지만 아직도 간헐적인 발병이 존재해 왔다.

해설_ **be wiped out**(사라지다)과 **though**(~에도 불구하고)에서 힌트를 얻을 수 있다. 따라서 '거의 사라지다'와 대치되는 의미인 **sporadic**(간헐적인)이 적절하다.

어휘_ **polio** 소아마비 **practically** 실제적으로, 거의 **wipe out** 철저히 파괴시키다, 없애버리다, 멸종시키다 **imminent** 임박한 **commencing** 시작하는

정답_ (b)

39.

해석_ 하수 오물은 부패하고 물은 악취를 풍기기 시작할 것이다.

해설_ 하수 오물(**sewage**)이 부패하면 물(**water**)은 악취(**odor**)를 '풍길' 것이므로, '(증기, 빛, 냄새 따위를) 내다, 풍기다, 발하다'는 뜻인 **give off**가 적절하다.

어휘_ **sewage** 하수, 오물 **decay** 썩다, 부패하다 **odor** 악취(*cf.* **smell**은 코로 지각되는 모든 냄새, **fragrance**는 꽃향기, **aroma**는 커피향 같은 은은한 향기) **take hold of** 붙잡다 **succumb to** ~에 굴복하다

정답_ (d)

40.

해석_ 그 회사는 물을 첨가함으로써 품질이 떨어진 우유를 판매했다는 이유로 고발되었다.

해설_ **adulterate** 섞음질해서 품질을 떨어뜨리다

어휘_ **be accused of** ~으로 인해 고발되다 **condense** 압축시키다 **enrich** 풍요롭게 하다, 윤택하게 하다

정답_ (d)

41.

해석_ 그는 비록 가정을 가진 어른이었지만 유아적인 처신을 하면서 자기 마음대로 되지 않으면 요란하게 주목을 끌었다.

해설_ infantile 유아적인

어휘_ grown man 어른(grownup) clamor for 요란하게 ~을 요구하다 get one's way 마음대로 하다 inoffensive 불쾌하지 않은 eclectic 절충적인 estranged 사이가 멀어진, 소원한

정답_ (a)

42.

해석_ 바이올린 연주 능력에 대한 나의 자신감은 지난 번 연주회에서 청중들에게 감명을 주지 못함으로 해서 여지없이 허물어졌다.

해설_ undermine 밑바닥을 허물어뜨리다, 근본을 파괴하다, (명성 등을) 훼손시키다

어휘_ confidence 신뢰, 자신감 fail to do ~하지 못하다 impress 깊은 인상을 심어주다, 감명을 주다 loosen 느슨하게 하다 sabotage 파괴하다

정답_ (a)

43.

해석_ 그 주지사는 정치적 장수의 단점들을 언급하면서, 자신의 임기가 연장된 후 유권자들이 모든 것에 대해 주지사에게 탓을 돌리는 데 점점 익숙해지게 되었다고 말했다.

해설_ longevity 장수

어휘_ comment on ~에 대해 언급하다 disadvantage 단점 extended tenure 연장된 임기 grow used to 점점 익숙해지게 되다 blame 탓하다, 책임을 전가하다 decorum 예절, 법도 debate (찬반 양론의) 토론

정답_ (d)

44.

해석_ Eileen의 독설과 급한 성미 때문에 그녀의 모욕적인 언사는 싸움을 불러일으키게 될 것이 틀림없다.

해설_ inevitable 불가피한

어휘_ insulting remarks 모욕적인 언사들 incidental 부수적인

정답_ (c)

45.

해석_ 러시아는 라트비아 근처의 파이프라인에서 기름이 유출된 것이 토양을 오염시켰다고 주장했다.

해설_ leak 누출되다

어휘_ urge 주장하다 contaminate 오염시키다

정답_ (a)

46.

해석_ 그는 자신이 저지른 실수를 깨닫고는 명예를 다시 찾기를 원했다.

해설_ redeem oneself 명예를 회복하다

어휘_ retain 유지하다, (변호사를) 고용하다 retail 소매하다 relish 맛을 느끼다

정답_ (c)

47.

해석_ 점점 많은 피해자들이 그들이 당한 부당한 것을 바로잡기 위해 소송하기로 결정했다.

해설_ '(잘못 따위를) 고치다, 교정하다'는 의미의 redress가 적절하다.

어휘_ litigation 소송 embrace 포옹하다 sue 고소하다 mark 표시하다

정답_ (b)

48.

해석_ 그 회사는 파산했다. 그 결과로 내 남편은 실직하게 되었다.

해설_ be made redundant는 주로 어쩔 수 없는 환경에 의해 해고되는 경우를 말한다.

어휘_ bankrupt 파산 unbounded 무한한 affirmative 확정적인

정답_ (c)

49.

해석_ 다음에 비행기에 탔을 때 눈이 마르고 두통이 나더라도 항공기의 환풍 시설을 탓하지 마세요. 이것의 실제 범인은 당신 몸의 기름과 상층 대기의 오존의 상호작용입니다.

해설_ don't blame과 the real에서 힌트를 얻을 수 있다. 비행 중 두통과 안구 건조를 항공기의 환풍 시설 탓으로 돌리지 말라(don't blame)며 진짜 원인을 설명할 것임을 유추할 수 있다. 따라서 the real 다음에는 '범인'을 뜻하는 culprit가 적절하다.

어휘_ ventilation system 환풍 시설 interaction 상호작용 atmosphere 대기 reference 참조 inference 추론 mission 임무

정답_ (a)

50.

해석_ 미군 부대는 식량의 부족으로 고통 받고 있는 반면, 독일 부대는 탄약을 무한정 공급받았던 것 같다.

해설_ inexhaustible 없어지지 않는. 나머지 어휘는 '부족함'의 의미를 가진 단어들이다.

어휘_ insufficient 불충분한 deficient 결핍되어 있는 wanting 부족한

정답_ (c)

Final Test (4)

1.

해석_ A: 참여자들 모두를 위해서 점심을 준비하기엔 시간이 너무 없어요.

B: 걱정 말아요. 그들 모두가 여기서 먹지는 않을 테니깐요.

해설_ 모든 참가자들을 위한 식사라고 하는 것으로 보아서, 요리 자체를 할 시간보다는 식사 준비의 시간 개념으로 보아야 한다.

어휘_ participant 참가자 cook 요리하다

정답_ (c)

2.

해석_ A: 당신이 말하려던 좋은 소식이 뭐죠?

B: 이제 회사 간부 취임식을 했으니 내가 당신 상사가 되었다는 거죠.

해설_ take on the mantle of ~에 취임하다

정답_ (d)

3.

해석_ A: 오, 이런 다행이! 전쟁터 한 가운데서 이렇게 안전하고 건강하게 돌아왔구나.

B: 정말이지 구사일생으로 살아돌아왔어요.

해설_ a narrow escape 구사일생

어휘_ sorrow 슬픔 shallow 얄팍한 hollow 텅 빈

정답_ (c)

4.

해석_ A: 왜넌 이 일을 그만두려고 안달이야?

B: 왜냐하면 내 상사 때문에 내 삶이 계속 비참했거든.

해설_ 상사(boss)가 자신의 삶을 miserable(비참한, 불행한)하게 만들어서 일을 그만두려고 안달이 난 것이다.

어휘_ be bent upon ~에 마음이 쏠리다 misery (복수형) 불행, 비참한 신세

정답_ (a)

5.

해석_ A: 난 이 여성이 이 지역의 농촌 사람들을 위해서 병원을 만들자고 생각해낸 제일 첫 번째 사람이라고 들었어.

B: 그뿐만이 아니야. 그 사람은 또한 이 마을 사람들의 건강관리를 위해서 농가 사람들이 공동 진료소 설립에 참여하도록 하는 아이디어를 앞장서서 실천했다구.

해설_ pioneer 개척하다, 선도하다, 지도하다

어휘_ rural 시골의 establish 설립하다 possess 소유하다

pray 기도하다

정답_ (c)

6.

해석_ A: 그거 들었어? 모두 그 이야기뿐이야. 사장이 새 비서와 바람이 났대.

B: 응. 그 이야기가 삽시간에 퍼지고 있어.

해설_ spread like wildfire (소문 따위가) 삽시간에 퍼지다

어휘_ have an affair 바람을 피우다

정답_ (d)

7.

해석_ A: 그를 여러 번 초대했지만, 그는 파티에 오지 않았어.

B: 알잖아, 그는 좀처럼 사람들과 어울리지 않는다는 거. 그는 매우 비사교적이야.

해설_ unsociable 비사교적인

어휘_ unsatisfied 불만족스런 unselfish 이기적이지 않은

정답_ (b)

8.

해석_ A: Joe가 상사에 대해 불평을 하는 이메일들을 상당히 많이 보냈는데 누군가가 그 메일들을 상사한테 전송했대.

B: 이제 Joe 큰일났구만!

해설_ be in hot water는 '곤경에 처하다'는 뜻이다. 아울러 get fired는 '해고당하다', hot potato는 '다루기 어려운 문제'를 의미한다는 것도 알아두자.

어휘_ complain 불평하다 forward 전달하다, 전송하다

정답_ (a)

9.

해석_ A: 있지, 이제 집에 가봐야돼. 공부할 게 많거든.

B: 아이, 너무 그러지 마! 공부는 나중에 해도 돼. 이번에는 Tim이 살 거야. 뭐 마실래?

해설_ '이어서 이번에는 ~가 산다'고 할 때는 buy the next round 라고 한다. (c)의 treat은 동사로 '한턱내다'란 의미인데, 명사로 이런 의미로 쓰일 때는 It's my treat.(내가 한턱내는 거야.)과 같은 형태로 굳어져 쓰이므로 빈칸에 적절치 않다.

어휘_ bill 청구서

정답_ (a)

10.

해석_ A: 아, 싫다. 또 집세를 내야 될 때네. 한 달이 정말 빨리 간다, 안

그래?

B: 그러게 말이야. 당장 한 푼도 없는데. 돈이 다 어디로 새어나가

는지 모르겠어.

해설 be broke 무일푼이다

어휘 impoverish 가난하게 하다 deprive 빼앗다

정답 (d)

11.

해석 A: 나 오늘 시험이 있어. 수업 시간에 배운 걸 다시 읽어봤어야 했

는데. 정말 걱정이야.

B: 시험을 보려면 복습이 중요한데, 너는 이번 주에 밤마다 놀러

나갔잖아.

해설 re-read에서 힌트를 얻을 수 있다. 시험에 대비해서 '복습' 한다

는 의미의 revise가 적절하다.

어휘 precautious 신중한 preview 예비조사, (영화 등의) 예고편

devise 고안하다, 계획을 세우다

정답 (d)

12.

해석 A: 와, 정말 멋진 선물이에요. 어떻게 감사해야 하죠, Jones 씨?

B: 우선 딱딱한 격식은 그만 차리죠. Tom이라고 불러요.

해설 자신을 Mr.Jones라고 격식을 차려 부르자 그냥 Tom이라 불

러달라고 부탁하는 것에서 유추할 수 있다. 따라서 '버리다', '그만

두다' (drop) 뒤에는 '격식'을 뜻하는 formality가 오는 것이 적

절하다.

어휘 courteous 예의바른 formalization 형식화, 의례화

hypocrisy 위선

정답 (a)

13.

해석 A: 며칠 전에 초밥을 먹은 뒤부터 몸이 안 좋아요. 아직도 배가 아

프고 어지러워요.

B: 그러세요. 다른 증세는 없나요?

해설 병원에서 벌어지는 대화. A는 자신의 배탈 '증세'를 설명하고 있

다. 이에 대한 B의 응답인 Any other ______?는 '다른 증상은

없나?'는 의미가 되어야 알맞다. 따라서 '증상, 증세'를 뜻하는

symptoms가 빈칸에 적절하다.

어휘 upset (배가) 아픈 feel dizzy 어지럽다 sentimental 감상

적인 sense 감각 complaint 불평

정답 (b)

14.

해석 A: 이제 신발 보러 갈까?

B: 그래, 보고나면 배가 고파지겠지, 그럼 뭐 좀 가볍게 먹으러

가자.

해설 peckish는 구어로 '배고픈' 이란 의미이다.

어휘 depressed 낙담한, 의기소침한 soberly (술 취지 않고) 말

짱한 정신으로

정답 (a)

15.

해석 A: 어떻게 지냈어요?

B: 음, 여기 대학의 파트타임 과정에 막 등록했어요. 아직 어학원

수업도 듣고 있고요.

해설 register는 '등록하다', apply와 file은 '신청하다'의 의미를

갖지만 전치사 for를 필요로 하므로 빈칸에 적절치 않다.

정답 (b)

16.

해석 A: 그 사람에게 세를 놓기를 원하신다면 집세를 좀 깎아주셔야 할

거예요.

B: 글쎄, 가격을 좀 내려줄 수는 있을 것 같은데요. 그런데 다른 세

입자들한테는 뭐라고 하죠?

해설 discount에서 힌트를 얻을 수 있다. '할인, 절감'을 뜻하는

reduction이 정답.

어휘 deduction 공제 thrifty 절약하는 augmentation 증가,

증대

정답 (b)

17.

해석 A: 당신은 지금 충분한 증거도 제시하지 않고 상당히 강력하게 주

장하고 계신데요. 확실한 증거를 정말로 갖고 있습니까?

B: 그거야 경찰이 갖고 있겠죠. 범인을 체포하는 건 시간문제일 뿐

이라고 확신해요.

해설 빈칸 뒤의 문장에서 hard evidence(확실한 증거)는 없는지 묻

고 있는 것으로 보아 allegation(충분한 증거가 없는 주장이나 탄

원)이 정답임을 알 수 있다.

어휘 conviction 유죄 판결 fraud 사기, 사기꾼 approval 승인,

시인

정답 (a)

18.

해석 A: 정말 감사합니다. 사기꾼, 거짓말쟁이, 도둑으로 낙인찍혔었는

데 덕분에 누명을 벗게 됐습니다.

　　B: 뭘요. 진실은 밝혀지기 마련이라고 하잖아요.

해설_be trapped는 '덫에 걸리다, 함정에 빠지다'의 의미가 있지만 뒤의 명사들과 연결이 안 된다. 문맥상 '낙인 찍힌'이란 의미의 **branded**가 적절하다.

어휘_trapped 갇힌, 덫에 걸린　**honor** 숭배하다

정답_(c)

19.

해석_A: 그동안 공부를 등한시했어. 다시 본분에 충실하고 싶어.

　　B: 그거 좋은 소식이다. 뭐 때문에 마음이 바뀌었니?

해설_distract는 **distracted from**으로 쓰이면 가능하다.

어휘_distract 마음, 주의를 딴 데로 돌리게 하다　**devote** 전념하다

정답_(c)

20.

해석_A: 아. 그럼 그 앤 그 사고에서 다친 게 아니었구나.

　　B: 아니야. 태어날 때부터 불구였어. 다행히 그 사고에선 병원 신세를 면했지.

해설_a born cripple은 '태어나면서부터 불구인 사람'을 뜻하는 관용표현이다. 참고로 **injured** 앞에 **the**를 붙여 **the injured**라고 하면 '부상자'를 뜻한다는 것도 알아두자.

어휘_avoid 피하다　**injured** 부상당한

정답_(c)

21.

해석_A: 어젯밤에 **Claire** 집에 도둑이 들었다는 얘기 들었어요?

　　B: 정말요? 나는 밤에 나갈 때는 집에 보통 불을 켜둬요. 그럼 도둑이 집에 들어올지 말지 다시 한 번 생각해보게 될 것 같거든요.

해설_burglar 강도, 도둑, (특히) 밤도둑. 문맥상 '도둑'을 뜻하는 단어가 적절하다.

어휘_be robbed 도둑맞다　**break in** ~에 침입하다　**poacher** 밀렵꾼　**shoplifter** 상점 들치기　**smuggler** 밀수업자

정답_(b)

22.

해석_A: 내가 거기로 갈게. 그런데 대략 10시에서 2시 사이가 될 거야.

　　B: 좀 더 구체적으로 할 순 없어? 하루 종일 기다릴 순 없잖아.

해설_I can't wait all day.라는 표현에서 B가 조금 더 '구체적인' 시간을 원하는 것을 알 수 있다. 따라서 **specific**이 적절하다.

어휘_specimen 표본　**speculative** (정보나 사실 확인 없이) 추측에 근거한

정답_(d)

23.

해석_A: 식당에서 나올 때 신용카드를 어디에 두었는지 기억이 안나.

　　B: 은행에 당장 신고해.

해설_report 신고하다

어휘_credit card 신용카드　**confirm** 확인하다

정답_(b)

24.

해석_A: 죄송하지만 이 부서에는 그런 이름을 가진 사람이 없습니다. 전화를 잘못 거신 것 같아요.

　　B: 아, 정말 미안합니다.

해설_have the wrong number 전화를 잘못 걸다

어휘_by that name 그런 이름으로 불리는, 그런 이름을 가진　**department** (직장 내) 부서　**sinister** 불길한, 사악한

정답_(a)

25.

해석_A: 업자를 고용하기 전에 사전에 가격을 알아보러 발품 좀 팔아 봤니?

　　B: 그럼, 사실 난 견적을 세 개 받아서, 그 중에서 중간 것으로 결정했어.

해설_shop around 상품[상점]을 보고 다니다, 가격을 알아보다

어휘_estimate 견적서

정답_(a)

26.

해석_ 그 위기는 정부가 무모하게 전쟁으로 치닫는 결정을 내렸기 때문에 야기됐다. 사람들은 가까운 미래에 벌어질 일에 대해 두려워하지만 당연한 것으로 받아들이고 있다.

해설_inexorably 중단할 수 없게

어휘_crisis 위기　**reckless** 무모한　**interferingly** 방해하면서　**interestingly** 흥미롭게도　**pursuantly** ~에 따라서, ~에 준해서

정답_(c)

27.

해석_ 법에 따르면 "소방법의 규정을 위반하면 구금이나 벌금형에 처한다"고 되어 있기 때문에 위반자는 투옥될 수도 있다.

해설_infringement 위반, 침해

어휘_offender 위반자, 범죄자　**obedience** 복종

confinement 감금 submission 순종, 중재, 제안

정답_ (c)

28.

해석_ 우리가 미네랄을 섭취하면 아미노산과 결합되어야 흡수된다.

해설_ ingest 섭취하다

어휘_ be combined with ~과 결합되다 amino acid 아미노산
absorb 흡수하다

정답_ (a)

29.

해석_ 은메달에는 통치자의 얼굴과 뛰어난 봉사에 대한 치하의 말이 새겨
져 있다.

해설_ inscription 비명, 비문

어휘_ sovereign 통치자 distinguished 현저한 subtle 미묘한

정답_ (a)

30.

해석_ 개인이나 단체가 지급 불능이면 빚을 갚을 충분한 돈이 없는 상태
를 말한다.

해설_ does not have enough money인 상태이므로 지급 불능
의 상태를 뜻하는 insolvent가 적절하다.

어휘_ debt 빚 abundant 풍부한 declaration 선언

정답_ (b)

31.

해석_ 지난 48시간 동안에 걸친 폭력 사태는 전직 비밀경찰에 의해 유발
되었다.

해설_ instigate 교사하다, 유발시키다

어휘_ trespass 남의 재산(땅)을 침범하다   infeasible 실행 불가
능한

정답_ (a)

32.

해석_ 그녀는 감옥에 있는 그녀의 남편에게 편지를 보냈는데 남편이 받기
전에 그 편지는 비밀 기관에 의해 가로채였다.

해설_ intercept 도중에서 가로채다

어휘_ delay 미루다 obstruct (물리적으로) 방해하다 seal 봉하다

정답_ (a)

33.

해석_ 캐나다는 기존의 시크교도들 간의 혼동을 막기 위해 이민을 희망하

는 시크교도들은 성씨를 개명해야 한다는 10년이 된 정책을 취소시
켰다.

해설_ a decade-old 때문에 pass가 될 수는 없다. 정책을 취소한다
는 의미의 nix가 적절하다.

어휘_ decade-old 10년 된 prospective 장래의

정답_ (b)

34.

해석_ 기독교도들의 상업적 거래에 대해서 종교세를 부과해야 한다고 주
장하는 사람들이 있다. 그들은 또한 이러한 상업적 거래는 종교적
인 것과 관계가 없다고 주장한다.

해설_ levy (세금을) 부과하다

어휘_ transaction 거래 exempt 면제하다 immunize 예방접
종을 실시하다 remit 송금하다, 경감하다

정답_ (d)

35.

해석_ 많은 이들이 이 법안에 반대하고 있기 때문에 만약 의원들의 투표
가 통과된다면 좋지 못한 결과가 있을 수 있다는 것에 대한 경고를
의원들은 받았다.

해설_ 법안(bill)이 많은 반대(oppose)에도 불구하고 통과(go
through)된다면 그에 따른 '결과'를 예상하여야 할 것이므로 빈
칸에는 '영향, 파문'을 뜻하는 repercussion이 적절하다.

어휘_ bill 법안 congress 국회 commencement 시작
deficiency 부족 causation 인과관계

정답_ (c)

36.

해석_ 국내 시장이 포화 상태가 됨에 따라 기업들은 해외로 수출을 할 필
요가 있다.

해설_ become saturated 포화되다

어휘_ domestic 국내의 abundant 풍부한 prevailed 널리 퍼
진, 우세한 underage 미성년의

정답_ (a)

37.

해석_ 음악업계에서는 더 수지가 맞는 mp3를 위해서 수지가 맞지 않는
컴팩트 디스크를 점진적으로 포기할 것이다.

해설_ lucrative 유리한, 수지맞는

어휘_ industry 산업 gradually 점차 abandon 버리다
manufacturing 제조 unprofitable 수지가 맞지 않는

정답_ (b)

38.

해석_ 정찰병이 돌아오자 장군은 적진이 어딘지를 정확하게 파악했다.

해설_ **pin down** 정확히 파악하다

어휘_ **simmer** 부글부글 끓다

정답_ (b)

39.

해석_ 우리가 힘을 합친다면, 여전히 이길 수 있는 기회가 있다.

해설_ **stick together** 힘을 합치다

어휘_ **stiffen** 경직시키다   **cement** (우정 따위의) 유대를 강화하다

정답_ (b)

40.

해석_ 보안카메라 회사들은 다음과 같이 선전했다. "무장한 시민들은 범죄를 예방하고 생명을 구합니다."

해설_ **crime**을 방지한다는 의미의 **deter**가 적절하다.

어휘_ **diffuse** (빛 따위를) 발산하다

정답_ (c)

41.

해석_ 폭력으로 사람의 생명을 앗아가는 것은 극악무도한 범죄이어서, 사형으로 벌하는 것이 적절하다.

해설_ **hideous** 무시무시한

어휘_ **death penalty** 사형 **deleterious** 유독한 **impudent** 뻔뻔스러운 **prudential** 분별 있는, 조심성 있는

정답_ (c)

42.

해석_ 아시아에서 일어나고 있는 현재의 금융 위기는 아시아 경제가 높이 나는 연과도 같이 그것의 본질적 힘이 아니라 바람과 실에 달려 있다는 것을 보여준다.

해설_ **wind**, **string**에 비추어 **flying** 다음에 올 명사는 **kites**가 되는 것이 적절함을 알 수 있다.

어휘_ **turmoil** 소란 **intrinsic** 본질적인

정답_ (b)

43.

해석_ 평범한 공원들과는 달리, 식물원과 수목원은 단순한 조경상의 아름다움 이상의 것을 염두에 두고 설계된다.

해설_ **arboretums** 수목원

어휘_ **ordinary** 보통의, 흔한 **botanical** 식물의 **conservatory** 온실

정답_ (a)

44.

해석_ 당신에 대한 고발에 반증한다는 것은 그 고발이 사실이 아닌 이유를 진술하는 것이다.

해설_ **rebuttal** 항변

어휘_ **retraction** 취소, 철회 **compromise** 타협 **rebuke** 징계

정답_ (b)

45.

해석_ 더구나, 거장의 연주처럼 그 피아노 연주곡 소나타는 음악적인 면뿐만 아니라 이미지 면에서도 엄청난 것을 형성하고 있다.

해설_ **virtuoso** 음악의 대가

어휘_ **performance** 연주 **fiasco** 큰 실패 **fresco** 프레스코화

정답_ (a)

46.

해석_ 강철은 주철만큼 약하지 않다. 강철은 쉽게 깨지지 않는다.

해설_ **doesn't break as easily**에서 힌트를 얻을 수 있다. 따라서 **not** 뒤에는 '깨지기 쉬운' 을 뜻하는 **brittle**이 적절하다.

어휘_ **blunt** 무딘 **brisk** 활기찬

정답_ (d)

47.

해석_ 최근에 우리가 개발한 그 기술은 우리가 계속 이윤을 추구할 수 있는 경쟁력을 우리에게 안겨줄 것이다.

해설_ **competitive edge**는 '경쟁력'이란 의미의 숙어적 표현이다.

어휘_ **competitive** 경쟁적인

정답_ (b)

48.

해석_ '문화의 충격'은 사람들이 처음으로 새로운 나라나 세계의 다른 지역으로 여행할 때 느끼는 감정이다.

해설_ 다른 나라에 처음으로 **(for the first time)** 갔을 때에 느끼는 감정이므로 단순히 흥분**(excitement)**이나 호기심**(curiosity)**보다는 **culture shock**이 더욱 적절할 것이다.

어휘_ **melancholy feeling** 우울함 **curiosity** 호기심

정답_ (a)

49.

해석_ 나는 감사에서 부당하게 해고된 것에 대하여 분노를 표시했다.

해설_ 문맥상 부당 해고(being unfairly dismissed)에 대해 '분노를 표시했다(expressed my indignation)'는 의미가 되어야 타당하다.

어휘_ audit 감사(監査) gratitude 감사, 고마움

정답_ (a)

50.

해석_ 당신이 받은 교육이 당신이 이루고자 하는 목표에 필요한 지식을 제공한다는 것을 기억해야만 한다.

해설_ 교육(educaton)을 통해 자신의 목표(goal)를 '달성' 하게 되므로 빈칸에는 '도달, 달성' 을 뜻하는 attainment가 적절하다.

어휘_ education 교육 necessary 필요한

정답_ (c)